Pizza!

Pizza!

Delicious recipes for toppings
and bases for all pizza lovers

Pippa Cuthbert &
Lindsay Cameron Wilson

NEW
HOLLAND

Dedication
To our sisters – Anna, Sally, Lee and Jessie.

First published in 2006 by
New Holland Publishers (UK) Ltd
London • Cape Town • Sydney • Auckland

Garfield House
86–88 Edgware Road
London W2 2EA
www.newhollandpublishers.com

80 McKenzie Street
Cape Town 8001
South Africa

Level 1, Unit 4
14 Aquatic Drive
Frenchs Forest, NSW 2086
Australia

218 Lake Road
Northcote
Auckland
New Zealand

10 9 8 7 6 5 4 3 2 1

ISBN 1 84537 412 6

Senior Editor: Clare Hubbard
Editor: Anna Bennett
Design: Paul Wright
Photography: Stuart West
Food styling: Pippa Cuthbert and Lindsay Cameron Wilson
Production: Hazel Kirkman
Editorial Direction: Rosemary Wilkinson

Reproduction by Pica Digital PTE Ltd, Singapore
Printed and bound in China by C&C Offset

NOTE
The author and publishers have made every effort to ensure
that all instructions given in this book are safe and accurate, but
they cannot accept liability for any resulting injury or loss or
damage to either property or person, whether direct or
consequential and howsoever arising.

ACKNOWLEDGEMENTS
As always, many thanks to Camilla Schneideman at
Divertimenti (www.divertimenti.co.uk) and Lindy Wiffen at
Ceramica Blue (www.ceramicablue.co.uk) for their gorgeous
props. Many thanks to Stuart West for his beautiful
photographs and to all our friends and family who contributed in
countless ways to this book. And of course to Books for
Cooks, where all of this began.

Contents

Introduction

Pizza is many things to many people. To the people of Naples, pizza is a way of life. There are over 500 pizzerias amidst the city's dusty churches and cramped dwellings. Within each pizzeria are veteran bakers standing before large, beehive-shaped wood-fired ovens. From these ovens come the traditional thin, puffy, charred crusts topped lightly with ingredients, such as the simple pizza Margherita, which is covered with tomatoes, olive oil, mozzarella and basil. Legend has it that a chef in Naples created this colourfully patriotic pizza in 1889 when the Queen of Italy came to visit. Contrary to popular lore, however, pizza isn't an original Neapolitan idea; it's simply their interpretation of what the Greek, Romans and undoubtedly the Arabs had been doing for centuries. Nevertheless, it is an interpretation that has clearly been successful.

To many Americans, pizza is something quite different. Italian immigrants brought Naples-style pizzas to America just before the turn of the twentieth century, but its popularity there didn't fully take off until the end of the Second World War, when US troops came home looking for the cheap, flavoursome pizza they had tasted for the first time in Naples. According to Jeffrey Steingarten, the renowned American food writer and Neapolitan-American pizza aficionado, there are 61,269 pizzerias in America. Not all of these, however, can uphold the traditions – and standards – of Naples. Welcome the thick, deep-pan pizzas of Chicago. The garden-fresh, seasonal pizzas of California. The smoky, spicy pizzas of the South West. The thick and thin pizzas favoured on the East coast. There are even pizza fans, somewhere in the middle, who prefer the mass-produced, plastic cheese-topped, pepperoni-studded greasy creations from their local pizza chain. Yes, the pizza has morphed in countless directions in America. It's fast food. It's street food. It's frozen, it's fresh. Some take pizzas seriously. Others down a slice while watching football. There are some (unfortunately almost everyone I know) who eat pizza, almost exclusively, on the way home from the pub. They call it street meat.

But I'm not American. Nor is Pippa. America is just the perfect example of how a country can embrace a dish and shape it over time. Every country has its own variations, permutations and interpretations of the pizza. Some are good, others are shameful. The latter graced the dining-room table of every primary school birthday party I attended. No, middle Americans are not alone. You know the kind of pizza I'm talking about – bland white crust, tasteless tomato sauce and salty discs of pepperoni covered in a mound of "double" cheese – the rubbery stuff someone dared to call mozzarella. A little dough ball sat in the middle of these gargantuan pizzas. It kept the cardboard box from adhering to the sticky pizza during delivery.

As some say, you have to hit rock bottom before you can climb back up again. That's what we, two humble pizza lovers from separate ends of the globe, are here to do – to move the pizza onwards and upwards, yet all the while keeping an eye on the past.

To us, pizza means Friday night. That was when imaginations ran wild and creative combinations began. It means trips to Italy. Memories of *pizza marinara* emerging from wood-fired ovens. Folding it over and devouring it as fast as it was cooked. It means university. Cheap meals, quick nourishment, happy gatherings. It means barbecues, eating al fresco under the stars. Most of all, pizza means being given the opportunity to corral these memories into one collective book. Here you will find our favourite, eclectic, creative and classic recipes from our repertoire. Some purists, like the members of the *Associazione Vera Pizza Napoletana*, who set out to defend the original Neapolitan pizza from imitations, wouldn't wholly approve. Our second chapter, aptly called Classics (see pages 42–61), is devoted entirely to the pizzas of southern Italy. It would pass, we think, with flying – red, white and green – colours. The rest of the recipes veer, albeit thoughtfully, away. How can we not? I live in Canada, where tomatoes aren't always, shall we say, perfect. Pippa lives in London. She isn't harvesting and pickling capers from the *Capparis spinosa* shrub in her garden. We cook with what *we* have, with *our* seasons, and are inspired by unique flavour combinations and the incredible bounty of produce that is available to *us*. We're resourceful, much like the people of Naples. Ian Thomson, in Nikko Amandonico's *La Pizza*, explains: "During the hungry years of the Second World War, the city's seaside aquarium was ransacked by famished locals who boiled the tropical fish for a variety of unusual pizza and pasta dishes. Neapolitans give this resourcefulness a name – *l'arte di arrangiarsi*, the art of getting by."

We aren't starving, nor are we living amidst a war. But we are blessed with *l'arte di arrangiarsi*. We love to experiment, to pair unexpected ingredients together, to fuse flavours. But you can't look forward without remembering the past. All of our recipes are based on the traditional pizza-making methods. Proper techniques are established. Flavour combinations are unique, but ingredients are pure. A wood-fired oven is encouraged. Of course we don't have one ourselves, but we'd really love it if we did. Dreaming aside, for the bulk of the home cooks out there, we've provided plenty of scope for experimentation. There are many sauces and pizza bases to choose from, depending on taste and time. The foundations are here, but as always, there is room to manoeuvre. Where some Neapolitans might scoff, the esteemed late English cookery writer

Elizabeth David would hopefully approve. In 1954 *Italian Food* was first published in an attempt to provide a book for her English readers who had previously been "protected" from authentic versions of Italian cookery. "This is", wrote David in the 1963 introduction to the Penguin edition, "a book for those readers and cooks who prefer to know what the original dishes are supposed to be like, and to be given the option of making their own adaptations and alterations according to their tastes and circumstances."

Many years have passed since David wrote those words, but they still ring true today. No, the English are no longer making pizzas by topping crumpets with tomato purée and a slice of processed cheese, as they did to David's horror in the 1950s. But crumpet pizzas are a fine example of how individual interpretation free from any culinary tradition can be a recipe, for, well, disaster. If you set forth using *Pizza!* as your guide, disaster will definitely be averted. Tradition will be upheld, but creativity encouraged. So go forth, we ask, with wild, leavened abandon.

Ingredients

PIZZA BASES

You can get great satisfaction from making your own pizza bases. Not only is the kneading process a great way to relieve stress but the end result will also taste better than any bought alternative! It is important, when making bread, to understand your ingredients in order to achieve the best result possible within your limitations. Environmental factors such as temperature and humidity will all play a part, as will the age of your flour, the hardness of your water and the freshness of your yeast. One single bread-making experience will never be the same as the next. Understand your dough and follow your instincts. If it feels a little dry then add more liquid early on; if it is too wet then add a little more flour. As always, our recipes are not set in stone. With practice you will become more aware of the signs to look out for and you will always end up with a soft and silky dough. If you are pressed for time, we do offer alternatives to making your own base (see page 15), which can make your pizza-making experience quick and very user-friendly without the extra flour mess!

PIZZA DOUGH MAKING

Mixing – this involves the mixing together of flour, water and yeast – as simple as that. At this stage the gluten proteins begin to unfold and form water-protein complexes. Secondly, the yeast begins to feed on the sugars and starts the process of fermentation and the production of carbon dioxide. In some of our recipes we use the "sponge" method, which involves mixing up to half of the flour in with the yeast and water mixture. This can give a slightly more aerated end product due to the longer time of fermentation.

Kneading – this improves the aeration of the dough and furthers the development of the gluten. It is best done by hand if you prefer a product with larger air bubbles but some bread machines and food mixers these days do have dough hooks, which will result in a very fine, cake-like texture. Your technique for kneading will determine the final texture of your bread or base. Your dough is well kneaded when it takes on a silky, satiny appearance. Rich, buttery or sweet doughs generally require longer kneading than others.

Rising (fermentation) – the stage when the dough is set aside and covered with a clean tea towel in a warm place. The gluten development is still happening but the main activity is the multiplication of yeast cells, which causes the dough to rise and expand. The yeast is producing more carbon dioxide, which in turn expands the air pockets resulting in the final texture. The dough should approximately double in size and then it is ready. At this stage it is important to punch the dough back to release the pressure, shape it and leave it for a further short rising. Then it is ready to be rolled out and topped.

Baking – when the dough is initially put in the oven it will experience a sudden expansion as the heat will cause a rapid production of carbon dioxide. When the interior of the dough reaches about 60°C (140°F) the yeast cells will die and the rising will cease. The dough will then undergo a phase of browning which will give the dough its crispy texture. The perfectly-cooked dough should sound hollow when tapped.

FREEZING DOUGH
Your dough can be frozen as individual balls after the rising (fermentation) stage. Just knock the dough back, reshape into a ball and place in a freezer bag. Remove the dough from the freezer about 6–8 hours before you need it. Leave it to defrost at room temperature. When you are ready, turn the plastic bag inside out and, using a floured hand, pull the dough from the bag. Knead the dough on a lightly floured surface for 5 minutes. Shape into a ball and leave for 20 minutes before rolling out.

FLOUR

There are two main types of wheat grown today, hard and soft, each with a characteristic kernel composition and each with its own particular culinary use. The wheat kernel will vary in "hardness", which is the measure of protein content and consequently determines the flour's gluten content. Hard flour contains large protein chunks and relatively little starch. As a result this flour forms a strong gluten when mixed with water and is commonly used in bread making. In comparison soft flours contain a higher starch content and consequently develop a weaker gluten. Soft flours are more commonly used for pasta and cakes where the texture is meant to be more tender and crumbly. Gluten works rather like chewing gum. It is both plastic and elastic, that is it will both change its shape under pressure and tend to reassume its original shape when pressure is removed. Gluten stretches when worked and allows air to be incorporated and trapped, resulting in air bubbles. Bread making requires a hard flour in order for the carbon dioxide, released by the yeast, to be incorporated by the gluten, enabling the dough to rise. Pizza dough does not require the same level of rising action as a loaf

of bread and many people claim that a softer flour is actually better. The following is a guide to the different flours available and their uses.

Semolina – a coarse grain produced from the hardest kind of wheat grown today. This is predominantly used for very stiff doughs, particularly dried pastas. It is too hard for bread or pasta making but can be added to pizza doughs for texture and crunch.

Hard flour – grade 1 contains the highest gluten level and is generally used for bread making or pizzas.

Soft flour – grade 00 (*doppio zero*) is the finest grade and contains less gluten. Useful for pasta making and baking. Soft flour can be used for pizza making but make sure the packet states that it is "panifiable".

YEAST

Yeasts are a group of single-celled fungi and about 160 different species are known. It is one species in particular, *Saccharomyces cerevisiae* or "brewer's sugar fungus", that is good for brewing and baking. Yeast gives off a characteristic flavour and smell; it leavens bread and converts the grain carbohydrates into alcohol and carbon dioxide. When we buy yeast it is live but inactive. With a little warmth and the addition of some water it is activated and releases the gas, carbon dioxide, that will raise the dough. The activity ceases only when the dough is placed in the oven and the yeast is killed by extreme heat.

Fresh yeast – this should be putty-like in colour and texture; it should look firm and moist and feel cool to the touch. If it is dry, dark and crumbly it may be stale or not live. Fresh yeast can be bought for a pittance from many supermarkets that have a bakery on site or from your local bakery. Keep fresh yeast in an airtight container in the fridge for up to 3 days. Alternatively, divide the yeast into 15-g or 30-g (½-oz or 1-oz) portions and freeze for up to 3 months. Always defrost your yeast thoroughly at room temperature or in the fridge before use.

To use: using a spoon, crumble the fresh yeast into a small glass bowl and add about a quarter of the required amount of water as specified in the recipe to it. Use the back of the spoon to cream the yeast until it dissolves in the water and forms a smooth blended paste. Stir in the remaining water. The yeast mixture is now ready to be added to the flour.

Dried granular yeast – usually bought in jars or tins from the supermarket. Dried yeast can be reconstituted with a little lukewarm water and will give exactly the same result as fresh yeast. It must be stored in an airtight container and always keep an eye on the date stamp. If it doesn't produce a frothy head when reconstituted with water it is not fresh.

To use: sprinkle dried granular yeast into a small glass bowl containing the quantity of lukewarm water as specified in the recipe. Leave to dissolve for 5–10 minutes. Once the yeast has dissolved, stir the mixture with a wooden spoon. The yeast mixture is now ready to be added to the flour. Continue as instructed in the recipe.

Dried easy-blend yeast – the easiest of yeasts to use as it is just added to the flour, with the water added separately. Again, the end product will be just as superior as using fresh or granular yeast. Always check the date stamp to ensure freshness.

To use: sprinkle dried easy-blend yeast directly onto the flour. The yeast will activate once the liquid has been added. Continue as instructed in the recipe. Easy-blend yeast cannot be used for the "sponge" method (see page 28).

NOTES
• 15g fresh yeast = 2 tsp dried granular yeast = 2 tsp dried powdered yeast

• In the recipes we have used dried granular yeast and the method has been written to reflect this. If you want to use other types of yeast when making the recipes, refer back to these pages.

OLIVE OIL
We've used extra virgin olive oil in our recipes. Olive oils vary considerably in taste and strength. Choose one with a flavour you like. In some cases we use infused olive oils, such as chilli or basil oil.

Infused oils – you can buy these or make your own. To infuse oils, firstly wash and dry your chosen herb or spice and lightly bruise to release the flavour. Place the herbs or spices in a clean, sterilized jar or bottle and cover with warmed oil. Seal tightly and leave in a cool, dark place to infuse for about 2 weeks. Leave the herbs and spices in if you want a stronger flavour or a decorative look, otherwise strain. Use the oils within 2 months of initial bottling. Some suggested flavourings are basil, chilli, rosemary, thyme, tarragon, cardamom, star anise or cloves.

PIZZA BASE ALTERNATIVES

Pitta bread – use pitta breads to make mini or individual pizzas, which are great for the kids. Let them top their own and experiment with the ingredients.

Tortillas – these make a thin and crispy base. These can also be cooked in a frying pan and even topped with a second tortilla to make a quesadilla. Great served as a quick finger-food snack chopped into wedges.

Naan bread – choose an Indian-inspired topping, such as spinach and paneer cheese, and finish it off with an authentic naan bread base. This is a breadier alternative to tortillas.

Puff pastry – it's hard to say whether making a pizza with puff pastry is cheating or not. Most of us would call this a tart but it's basically the same concept and a quick and easy alternative if you buy ready-rolled sheets.

Bought bases – bought pizza bases come in many shapes and forms and are available from all good supermarkets. Try frozen, vacuum-packed or ready-rolled bases from the chiller cabinet. Some supermarkets or delicatessens may also sell frozen balls of pizza dough, which just require defrosting, and shaping. Alternatively, get friendly with your local Italian restaurant and they may sell you frozen balls of dough.

TOMATOES

There are over 5,000 varieties of tomato in the world today from yellow cherry tomatoes and green plum tomatoes to red beef tomatoes! It was in Naples that tomatoes transformed the original white pizza into the red, tomato-topped variety we know today. Italian cooking without the tomato would truly be unthinkable. Tomatoes can be bought in many varieties: fresh, tinned, puréed, sun-dried and semi-dried are all readily available today. Tomatoes are made up of about 94 per cent water and must always be well drained, whether fresh or tinned, in order to avoid a soggy pizza.

Tinned tomatoes – these are scalded, peeled and slightly salted before being tinned. Tinned tomatoes are a very popular choice for pizza makers today and are of equal quality to the fresh variety. In many cases it is the superior, unblemished tomatoes that are sent away for canning when the not so perfect tomatoes are left behind for fresh sale.

Tomato purée – many professional pizza makers steer clear of tomato purée, arguing that it tends to dull the other flavours, making all pizzas taste the same. We're not sure if this is truly the case and it is certainly a useful ingredient if you want to assemble a pizza in a hurry.

CHEESES
Mozzarella
Mozzarella di bufala is the original mozzarella and is delicious served as is. It is sweet in flavour and soft in texture but does not melt as well as cow's mozzarella. Cow's milk mozzarella is the one to use for cooking. It has a very mild, creamy and faintly sour flavour and melts beautifully, making it ideal for pizzas.

Mozzarella can also be made with goat's milk, which is a little sharper in taste and is not such a popular choice.

Mozzarella is produced as a semi-soft, fresh cheese or a firm block of cheese made with low- or non-fat milk. The fresh cheese is the ultimate choice for home-made pizzas but it is important to make sure you drain and dry it well to remove as much excess moisture as possible. Fresh mozzarella balls are usually packaged in water or, alternatively, brine or whey, to preserve freshness. Fresh mozzarella is mild in flavour, soft and very pliable. The longer mozzarella ages the softer and sourer it becomes. In all our recipes we have used fresh mozzarella balls unless otherwise specified.

Mozzarella can also be found in other forms:

Block mozzarella – block mozzarella is lower in moisture than fresh mozzarella and is often the preferred choice for many commercial pizza makers. In America as many as 90 per cent of all commercial pizza makers will use block mozzarella. It is lower in fat and consequently not as flavoursome as fresh mozzarella.

Bocconcini – small mozzarella balls usually about 2.5cm (1in) in diameter.

Mozzarella affumicata – *affumicato* means smoked in Italian. This cheese is lightly smoked over wood chips and is darker in colour than normal mozzarella.

Mozzarella scamorza – this mozzarella has been heavily smoked, usually over pecan shells, and is much darker in colour and denser in texture.

Mozzarella pearls – tiny balls of mozzarella, which are about 1.5cm (⅝in) in diameter. They are available from some supermarkets but if you can't find them then a large mozzarella ball cut into cubes does exactly the same thing.

Mozzarella can be wrapped in plastic food wrap and frozen for up to 3 months. Frozen mozzarella does decrease in flavour and may become moister in texture. Before serving or cooking allow the cheese to defrost in the fridge before removing and warming to room temperature. Fresh mozzarella usually keeps for up to 2 weeks in the fridge.

Parmesan
When buying Parmesan cheese always look for the words *Parmigiano reggiano* for authenticity and quality. Never buy pre-grated or shaved Parmesan in tubs. It is important to keep your Parmesan from drying out so always buy a freshly cut piece and grate only when needed. Parmesan cheese is rich and round in flavour and has the ability to melt with heat and become inseparable from the ingredients to which it is joined. To store your Parmesan for longer than 2–3 weeks divide it into pieces, each with a piece of rind still attached, and wrap tightly in greaseproof paper, then in heavy duty aluminium foil. Store on the bottom shelf of the fridge.

Pecorino
The Italian word for sheep is *pecora*, hence all cheese made

from sheep's milk is called pecorino. There are dozens of pecorinos available: some are soft and fresh while others are crumbly and sharp, more like a Parmesan.

Fontina
Fontina is a semi-hard cheese with a creamy texture and subtle nutty flavour. It is a very useful cheese for cooking as it has good melting properties, making it a popular choice in fondues and pizzas. Fontina is made from unpasteurized cow's milk from the grazing cows of the Val d'Aosta alpine region of Italy.

Ricotta
The word *ricotta* literally means "recooked" in Italian. It is made from the whey of other cheeses that is cooked again to make a milky white, soft, granular and mild tasting cheese. Ricotta does not melt.

Gruyère
Gruyère is a firm cheese with a nutty flavour. It works best when finely grated.

Asiago
A semi-firm to hard Italian cheese with a nutty, sharp flavour that is mainly used for grating. Asiago was traditionally made with sheep's milk, but it is now more commonly made with cow's milk.

Havarti
Havarti is a mild, semi-soft Danish cheese with small irregular holes.

Monterey Jack
Monterey Jack is a type of Cheddar-style cheese first made in California using pasteurized cow's milk. It is commonly sold by itself, or mixed with Colby cheese to make a marbled cheese known as Colby-Jack (or Co-Jack).

Cheddar
Choose a mature Cheddar for the best flavour and always grate for use on pizza to get a more even melt.

Provolone
This is a southern Italian cheese that is pale yellow in colour, with a smooth texture. Milder, fresh provolone can be eaten on its own, although once aged it is generally used in cooking.

Gorgonzola
Gorgonzola is a mild and creamy blue-veined cheese. Choose dolcelatte if you prefer a creamier, milder soft blue cheese.

Taleggio
Taleggio is a semi-soft cheese made from whole cow's milk. Its flavour can range from mild to pungent, depending on its age.

When young, the colour of taleggio is pale yellow. As it ages it darkens to deep yellow and becomes rather runny. Taleggio is sold in blocks and is covered either with a wax coating or a thin mould.

Mascarpone

Mascarpone is a soft, unripened cheese that belongs to the cream cheese family. It comes from northern Italy and is a thick, rich, sweet and velvety, ivory-coloured cheese produced from cow's milk that has the texture of sour cream. It is sold in plastic tubs and can be found in most delicatessens and good supermarkets.

CURED MEATS
Prosciutto

Prosciutto is the pig's hind thigh or ham that has been salted and air-dried. The salt draws off the meat's excess water, thus curing and preserving it. A true prosciutto is never smoked. When served it should always be thinly sliced and used as soon as possible. If you are not consuming it immediately then each slice or each single layer of slices must be covered with greaseproof paper or clingfilm then wrapped in aluminium foil. Prosciutto is delicious eaten as it is or cooked on pizzas. It can be quite salty so do not add extra salt unless needed.

Pancetta

Pancetta is from the pig's belly and is the Italian equivalent of bacon. Pancetta can be bought sliced or cubed and is more tender and considerably less salty than prosciutto. It can also be eaten raw or cooked. Pancetta is rarely ever smoked except in a few areas of northern Italy.

Salami

Salami is the generic term for cured and fermented meat (usually pork or beef) that is typically flavoured with spices such as black pepper, fennel, chilli or paprika. The meat mixture is ground and stuffed into casings then hung to dry, either in hot or cool air, until the sausages have reduced in weight by at least half. Some salamis or cured sausages will additionally be smoked. Examples of common salamis and cured sausages are Napoli, Milano, Genoa, chorizo and pepperoni.

Mortadella

Mortadella can be used sliced or diced on pizzas. It is made from the lean shoulder and neck meat from carefully selected pigs and is then studded with the creamy fat from other parts of the pig. Mortadella is often flavoured with a blend of spices and condiments that varies from producer to producer.

Bresaola

Bresaola is very thinly sliced, cured and air-dried lean beef. It is gently spiced to develop its rich and aromatic flavour.

Equipment

COOKING METHODS
The wood-fired oven
This is an essential factor in the creation of the true Neapolitan pizza. The design of the traditional wood-fired pizza oven is more than 2,000 years old. These ovens are dome-shaped, made from brick or clay, and the roof is heated by direct contact with the flames from the burning wood below. The dome shape then causes the heat to be reflected back down to the base of the oven.

In a well-used oven (such as those in many pizzerias in Naples) the fire will never go out completely – even when there are no pizzas in the oven. The flames will die right down and just embers will be left burning so the oven can be bought back up to temperature at a much faster rate. A pizza oven will reach about 400°C (750°F), at which temperature a pizza will cook in about 1½ minutes. If you are lucky enough to have a wood-fired oven the woods of choice are cherry or olive wood, as they don't smoke as much as other woods. Make sure you also invest in a long pizza paddle to get your pizzas in and out of the deep oven.

Wood-fired ovens are becoming more and more popular as an outside alternative to a barbecue. They are used to cook a wide variety of foods, not just pizzas. Whole large roasts and loaves of bread can be successfully cooked in them as well as semi-dried tomatoes, courgettes and other vegetables.

The electric oven
For a while electric ovens were beginning to replace the traditional wood-fired oven in many pizzerias around the world. It seems today that the wood-fired oven may be making a comeback in most pizzerias but for many of us an electric oven is still the main oven of choice. With an electric oven we have a lot more control over temperature and this makes it more suited to most domestic homes. Although the flavour and smell may not be quite as authentic as that of a wood-fired oven, the pizza that you will produce can still be of top quality. It may be worth investing in a pizza stone if you are planning on doing some serious pizza making at home (see opposite). All our recipes are tested

in fan-assisted ovens, which produce a crisper, golden crust.

The pizza stone

A pizza stone will transform your electric or gas oven into the modern equivalent of the clay and brick ovens used by traditional pizza bakers. Cooking pizzas on such a stone gives them a crispness that cannot otherwise be achieved from an oven. Most pizza stones have been fired at temperatures in excess of 1,100°C (2,000°F). This enables them to give a very dry heat that is also evenly distributed, eliminating any hot spots and giving a consistent browning to your pizza. Pizza stones are suitable for use in both gas or electric ovens. Try serving your pizza directly on the stone and it will stay hot right through until the last slice. It is important always to heat your pizza stone first so it can absorb the heat of the oven. You will need a pizza paddle (see page 24) or use our parchment paper technique (see page 24) to transfer your topped pizza quickly on to the stone without losing too much heat – alternatively, you will need to work very quickly to assemble your topping. Sprinkle a little flour on the pizza stone first to stop it sticking. Be very careful when handling the stone as it gets very hot and will remain hot for a long time.

In our recipes we have said to use a baking sheet as not everyone will have a pizza stone, but obviously if you have one use it instead.

The barbecue

Cooking pizza on the barbecue is a great way to impress your guests. It requires no special skills, just the flick of the switch or some burning coals. It's a good idea to keep a supply of frozen pizza dough balls in the freezer for those spontaneous summer evenings. Just defrost the dough (see page 11), roll it out and within minutes you can have a crisp, slightly charred crust with your chosen topping. Some topping ingredients, such as bunches of cherry tomatoes or grilled aubergines, are best cooked separately. Let the cheese melt on the base and throw the extra topping on – hey presto!

OTHER EQUIPMENT
Pizza paddle
If you own a wood-fired oven or a pizza stone then a pizza paddle is definitely worth investing in. Always lightly flour it before setting the dough on it so that it can easily be transferred to the oven or on to the pizza stone.

Thermometer
If you are lucky enough to own a wood-fired oven then a good thermometer is essential in order to judge the inside temperature of the oven. Choose one that reaches a temperature of at least 400°C/750°F.

Pizza plates
If you don't have a pizza stone on which to serve your pizza then you will need to buy a few flat, round plates for serving. Alternatively large chopping boards will suffice.

Pizza cutter
A pizza cutter definitely speeds up the cutting process.

Baking parchment
Baking parchment can be very useful to help transfer your topped pizza on to your baking sheet or pizza stone. Make sure the paper is lightly floured and just roll out your pizza dough on it as you would on any other surface. Slide the paper and dough onto the pizza stone or baking sheet and leave the paper there during cooking.

Ladle
Useful for transferring sauce from the bowl to the pizza base. Then use the base of the ladle to distribute the sauce around the base, ensuring you leave a 1–2-cm (½–¾-in) border. Most of our pizzas call for 125ml (4fl oz) sauce so try buying a ladle that fits this volume exactly.

RECIPE INFORMATION

• All pizza recipes make 1 pizza unless otherwise specified and generally serve 1–2 people.

• For all our recipes we have given our preferred choice of base and sauce. These are not set in stone and it is important to mix and match and experiment with different flavour combinations.

• All our recipes have been tested in a fan-assisted oven. If you are using a conventional oven then increase our recommended cooking temperature of 220°C/425°F/Gas mark 7 to 240°C/475°F/Gas mark 9. All ovens vary in performance so always check that your pizza is cooked to the desired crispness before serving.

• Keep your pizza toppings simple and the result will always be better.

• Unless otherwise stated, pizzas should always be served straight from the oven while the base is still crispy.

• Always use floured work surfaces and hands when working with pizza bases.

• In all our recipes we have used fresh mozzarella unless otherwise specified.

Bases and breads

Many say there is nothing better than the thin, puffy crust of a Neapolitan pizza. It is a beautiful thing, we know. But it's good to stretch the comfort zone. Try something new, experiment. Break free!

Pizza lovers in Chicago have certainly broken free. The cold windy winters call for thick, deep crusts with lots of toppings. Wet, substantial toppings and a thick layer of cheese call for a thick crust. The heat of the oven melds everything into the crust, fusing the two together into one, comforting mass. The weather calls for it, the body needs it.

Then there are those looking for speed. That's where our no-rise crusts come in. And for those with problems with gluten? There is something for them as well. Either way, simply compile, mix, roll and top. It's as simple as that. Making dough is perhaps the easiest experiment in breaking free imaginable.

Don't forget the sweet. Our honey-infused, saffron-scented crust will make you smile. Topped with sweet pears and walnuts, caramelized apples or simply served neat, dabbling in sweet territory will bring you, well, sweet success.

Crispy pizza base
Perfection

This dough uses the "sponge" method – some of the flour is added to the water and yeast, and the resulting "sponge" is allowed to rest before the remaining flour is mixed in.

Makes 4 x 25–30cm (10–12in) pizzas

4 tsp **dried granular yeast**
300ml (10fl oz) **lukewarm water**
500g (1lb 2oz) **plain flour**
1 tsp **salt**

Sprinkle the yeast into 100ml (3½fl oz) of the water. Leave to dissolve for 5–10 minutes. Add about 2 Tbsp of the flour and mix to a smooth paste then stir in the remaining water. Cover and leave the yeast mixture for about 30 minutes or until it is bubbling and foamy.

Combine the flour (reserve 2 Tbsp for kneading) and salt in a large bowl and make a well in the centre. Pour in the yeast liquid. Using a wooden spoon, work the ingredients together by pulling the flour into the liquid until it comes together.

Use your hands to transfer the mixture to a lightly floured surface. Knead the dough for 10 minutes or until it is smooth and elastic. Form the dough into a round loaf. Leave to rise under a clean tea towel for about 1½–2 hours or until doubled in size.

Punch down the dough and knead for a couple of minutes. Divide into four balls. Press each dough ball out flat and, using a floured rolling pin, shape into a 25–30cm (10–12in) diameter circle. Using your knuckles, press just inside the edges to raise them slightly. Leave to rest for 10–15 minutes. Preheat oven to 220°C/425°F/Gas mark 7.

Add your toppings. Cook in the middle of the oven for 10–12 minutes (unless otherwise instructed depending on the toppings) or until crispy and golden and the base is cooked.

Quick scone base

Simplicity

Try adding cayenne pepper or English mustard powder to the scone mixture for a more savoury note.

Makes 1 x 25cm (10in) pizza

250g (9oz) **plain flour or 00 flour**
1 tsp **baking powder**
1 pinch **salt**
30g (1¼oz) **butter (at room temperature),** cut into cubes
200ml (7–9fl oz) **milk**

Preheat the oven to 200°C/400°F/Gas mark 6. Sift and combine the flour, baking powder and salt in a large bowl. Add the cubes of butter and lightly rub into the flour until the mixture resembles the texture of breadcrumbs. Add the milk to the rubbed mixture and stir with a palette knife or metal spoon until it begins to come together. Finish it off with your hands – it should be soft but not sticky (if the dough seems too dry add a little more milk, a teaspoon at a time). The dough should come together and leave the sides of the bowl clean.

Shape the dough into a ball with your hands and transfer it to a lightly floured surface. Flour a rolling pin and roll the dough out to about 1cm (½in) thick and 25cm (10in) in diameter.

Place the round on a lightly floured baking sheet and top as required. Cook in the middle of the preheated oven for 12–18 minutes, depending on the topping, or until cooked and golden.

Thick-crust pizza base/calzone dough

Tender

Every so often the need strikes for a thick, luscious crust to sink your teeth into. This recipe will satisfy those needs!

Makes 4 x 30cm (12in) pizzas or 6 x 20–25cm (8–10in) calzoni

2 Tbsp **dried granular yeast**
500ml (18fl oz) **lukewarm water**
750g (1lb 10oz) **plain flour**
80g (3oz) **cornmeal or polenta**
2 tsp **salt**
125ml (4fl oz) **olive oil**

Sprinkle the dried granular yeast into the water. Leave to dissolve for 5–10 minutes.

Combine the flour, cornmeal and salt in a large mixing bowl. Make a well in the centre and slowly add olive oil and yeast mixture. Stir with a wooden spoon until the mixture is roughly combined. It will be quite moist.

Lightly flour a work surface and tip out the dough. Knead for 8–10 minutes, until smooth and elastic. Place the dough in a large, clean, oiled bowl, cover and leave to rise for 1 hour, or until doubled in size.

Preheat the oven to 220°C/425°F/Gas mark 7. Knead the dough again a few times, then divide it into four equal parts to make four 30-cm (12-in) pizzas, or six equal parts to make six 20–25-cm (8–10in) calzoni. Place on a lightly floured baking sheet.

Add your toppings and cook in the middle of the preheated oven for 14–16 minutes or until crispy and golden and the base sounds hollow when tapped.

Thick-crust pizza base/calzone dough

Pizza bites

Pizza bites

Inspirational

These little morsels make a great party canapé. Top them with whatever you like or keep them plain to dip into hummus or guacamole.

Makes 20–24

1 x 30-cm (12-in) **Crispy pizza base (see page 28)**
4 Tbsp **Coriander pesto (see page 164)**
4 Tbsp **cream cheese**
2 **spring onions**, sliced

To serve
Sweet chilli sauce
Coriander leaves

Preheat the oven to 220°C/425°F/Gas mark 7.

Prepare the pizza dough and roll it out to a 30-cm (12-in) round as you would if making one round pizza. Using a small metal pastry cutter, cut as many rounds from the dough as possible. Carefully transfer the rounds to a lightly floured baking sheet.

Prick each round once or twice with a fork. Top each round with about ½ tsp Coriander pesto and ½ tsp cream cheese. Sprinkle over 2–3 slices of spring onion and cook in the middle of the preheated oven for 6–8 minutes or until golden and crisp. Serve hot, warm or cold topped with sweet chilli sauce and coriander leaves.

Gluten-free quick pizza base

Soft

This base is very similar in flavour and texture to our Quick scone base (see page 29), but the addition of rice flour makes it friendlier to those with wheat allergies.

Makes 2 x 30cm (12in) thin crusts

175g (6oz) **brown or white rice flour**
1 Tbsp **caster sugar**
½ tsp **bicarbonate of soda**
½ tsp **salt**
225ml (8fl oz) **plain yogurt**

Preheat the oven to 180°C/350°F/Gas mark 6.

Combine the flour, sugar, bicarbonate of soda and salt in a large bowl. Add the yogurt and stir until roughly combined. Turn the dough on to a floured surface and knead for 1 minute, or until it comes together into a smooth ball. Form into two balls with your hands and transfer to a lightly floured surface. Flour a rolling pin and roll the dough to about 1cm (½in) thick and 25cm (10in) in diameter. Place onto a lightly floured baking sheet and top as required. Cook in the middle of the preheated oven for 12–15 minutes or until cooked and golden.

Grilled pizza base

Smoky

All that's needed to make this pizza is a barbecue with a lid, clear skies and appetites.

Makes 6 x 20cm (8in) pizzas

2 tsp **dried granular yeast**
275ml (10fl oz) **lukewarm water**
About 500g (1lb 2oz) **plain flour**
2 tsp **salt**
75ml (2½fl oz) **olive oil, plus extra for brushing**

Sprinkle the yeast into the water. Leave to dissolve for 5–10 minutes. Combine the flour and salt in a large bowl. Slowly add the yeast mixture and olive oil alternately, stirring with a wooden spoon after each addition. Turn out the dough on to a lightly floured work surface and knead for 8 minutes, until the dough is soft and elastic. Place the dough in a large, lightly oiled bowl and leave to rise until doubled in size, about 1 hour.

Punch down the dough and divide into six balls. Put each ball, one by one, on to a floured surface then flatten and shape into a circle with a rolling pin. Cover each circle with clingfilm and leave to rest for a further 5 minutes. Run the rolling pin over the circles again, until they are about 20cm (8in) in diameter. Use the rounds immediately, or layer them between pieces of baking parchment, cover and refrigerate for up to 4 hours.

Preheat the barbecue to high on one side, warm on the other. Brush one side of the base with oil. Place the base oiled-side down on the hot side of the barbecue. Grill until grill marks appear, 2–3 minutes. Turn the dough over and add toppings. When the bottom has browned, slide the pizza to the cooler side of the barbecue. Close the lid and grill until the toppings are hot and the cheese has melted.

Pesto flat breads

Finger food

These can be made using any of the pesto recipes on pages 162–165. Just follow exactly the same method substituting your favourite pesto.

Makes 1 flat bread

1 x 30-cm (12-in) **Crispy pizza base (see page 28)**
3 Tbsp **pesto of choice (see pages 162–165)**
3–4 **basil leaves,** torn
25g (1oz) **pine nuts,** toasted
Extra virgin olive oil, for brushing

Roll the pizza base so it is ready to be topped. Preheat the oven to 220°C/425°F/Gas mark 7.

Spread the pesto over half of the round, leaving a 1-cm (½-in) border uncovered around the edge. Sprinkle with the torn basil and pine nuts. Fold the uncovered side of the round over the filling and press the edges together to seal them. Using a sharp knife, make diagonal cuts through the top at 2-cm (¾-in) intervals, exposing the pesto mixture. Brush the dough with olive oil. Place on a lightly floured baking sheet and cook in the middle of the preheated oven for 10–12 minutes or until crispy and golden and the base sounds hollow when tapped.

Using a large knife or pizza cutter, cut the flat bread into strips using the diagonal cuts as a guide and serve immediately or at room temperature.

Pesto flat breads

Pizza breads

Pizza breads

Savoury

These are a great way to start a casual dinner party. Just make sure your guests don't fill up on pizza breads.

Makes 4 breads

1 quantity **Crispy pizza base dough (see page 28)**

Topping suggestions
- **Leaves from** 2 **rosemary stalks,** finely chopped + 1 tsp **sea salt** + 1 **clove garlic, crushed** + 2 Tbsp **extra virgin olive oil**
- 2 Tbsp **extra virgin olive oil** + 2 Tbsp **capers,** rinsed, drained and roughly chopped + 1 **clove garlic,** crushed + **ground black pepper**
- 1 Tbsp **chilli oil** + 1 tsp **thyme leaves** + 30g (1oz) **finely grated Gruyère cheese**
- **Sea salt + freshly ground black pepper** + 1 Tbsp **extra virgin olive oil** + 100g (3½oz) **mozzarella,** cubed
- 1 Tbsp **extra virgin olive oil** + 4 **anchovy fillets** + 1 **clove garlic,** all crushed together
- 2 Tbsp **pesto (see pages 162–165)** + 75g (2¾oz) **mozzarella**

Make the Crispy pizza base dough up to the point where you have four individual dough balls. Shape each ball into 25–30-cm (10–12-in) rounds, prick evenly four to five times with a fork and transfer to a baking sheet and rest for 10 minutes.

Preheat the oven to 220°C/425°F/Gas mark 7. For all toppings suggestions, combine all the ingredients, except the cheese (if using), and brush over the whole pizza base using a pastry brush. Then sprinkle over the cheese, if using. Cook in the middle of the oven for 8–10 minutes or until golden and crispy. Cut into wedges and serve immediately.

Focaccia pizza base

Airy

This is a substantial, but not-too-heavy pizza base.

Makes 2 x 25cm (10in) pizzas

2 tsp **dried granular yeast**
250ml (9fl oz) **lukewarm water**
500g (1lb 2oz) **plain flour**
1 tsp **salt**
3 Tbsp **olive oil**

Sprinkle the yeast into the water. Leave to dissolve for 5–10 minutes. Combine the flour (reserving about 2 Tbsp for kneading) and salt in a large bowl and make a well in the centre. Pour in the olive oil and yeasted water. Using a wooden spoon, work the ingredients together by pulling the flour into the liquid mixture until it comes together, adding a little additional water if necessary. Using your hands, transfer the mixture to a lightly floured surface. Knead the dough for 10 minutes or until it is smooth, silky and elastic in texture. Form the dough into a ball and put in a clean, lightly oiled bowl. Cover with a clean tea towel and leave to rise for about 1–1½ hours or until doubled in size.

Once doubled in size, knock the dough back and knead for a further 5 minutes. Cut the dough into two even-sized pieces, press out flat and, using a floured rolling pin, shape into about 25-cm (10-in) rounds. Cover again and leave to rest for a further 15–20 minutes.

Preheat the oven to 220°C/425°F/Gas mark 7. Using the tips of your fingers, make shallow indentations all over the surface of the dough. The dough is now ready to be topped. Cook on a lightly floured baking sheet in the middle of the oven for 14–16 minutes or until golden and the base is cooked through.

Sweet honey pizza base
Subtle

Sweet dough requires a little more kneading than savoury dough in order to get to the same silky, smooth texture.

Makes 2 x 30cm (12in)
  thick-crust bases or
  4 x 30cm (12in)
  thin-crust bases

2 tsp **dried granular yeast**
125ml (4fl oz) **lukewarm water**
175ml (6fl oz) **lukewarm full-cream milk**
175ml (6fl oz) **runny honey**
1 Tbsp **extra virgin olive oil**
1 **large egg,** beaten
Finely grated zest of 1 lemon
8g (¼oz) **saffron powder (optional)**
1 tsp **salt**
550–600g (1lb 4oz–1lb 5oz) **plain flour**

Sprinkle the yeast into the water. Leave to dissolve for 5–10 minutes. Add the milk, honey, oil, egg, lemon zest and saffron (if using) to the yeast mixture and stir well. Sift the salt and flour into the wet mixture and mix to a dough, adding additional flour if necessary to form a ball. Transfer the mixture to a lightly floured surface and knead for 10–15 minutes or until smooth and elastic. Return the dough to a clean bowl and leave covered for about 1½ hours or until doubled in size.

Knock the dough back and divide into two or four, depending on the desired thickness of the base required, and shape into 25–30-cm (10–12-in) rounds. Leave the dough to rest for 10–15 minutes.

Preheat the oven to 220°C/425°F/Gas mark 7. Add your toppings. Cook the pizzas in the middle of the oven for 10–12 minutes for a thin base or 15–18 minutes for a thicker base or until lightly golden and crispy.

Classics

In Naples there is only one pizza. It begins with the simple recipe of water, yeast, flour and salt. The water activates the yeast, the flour feeds it and the moist, warm air allows it all to grow. Experienced hands stretch it into a circle. Simple toppings such as tomatoes, fresh basil and mozzarella are scattered on top. A long wooden paddle inserts it into a domed-shaped wood-fired oven. Temperatures inside the oven range from 357°C (675°F) on the floor to 510°C (950°F) on the ceiling. Such temperatures will cook a pizza in 80 to 120 seconds. The crust is puffy and charred, thin yet chewy. It's simple yet specific. To a Neapolitan, it's the only way.

Pizza wasn't invented in Naples, or Italy for that matter. Nevertheless, the Neapolitan pizza, with its charred puffed-up crust and light, tomato-based toppings, is undoubtedly the best in the world. Out of respect for this simple fact, we bring you a chapter devoted entirely to the classic pizzas of Naples and its surrounding areas.

Marinara

Neat

This was the original, first-ever Neapolitan pizza – simplicity at its best!

Makes 1 pizza

1 x 30-cm (12-in) **Crispy pizza base (see page 28)**
200g (7oz) **cherry tomatoes,** halved
⅛ tsp **salt**
2 Tbsp **extra virgin olive oil**
1 **clove garlic,** thinly sliced
1 tsp **dried oregano**
Sea salt and freshly ground black pepper

Prepare the pizza base so it is ready to be topped. Preheat the oven to 220°C/425°F/Gas mark 7.

Halve the tomatoes and place in a sieve over a bowl. Press the tomatoes firmly with the back of a spoon to release as much liquid as possible. Sprinkle over the ⅛ tsp salt and leave to drain for a further 10 minutes. Brush the base with half of the olive oil. Scatter the cherry tomatoes over the pizza base, leaving a 1–2 cm (½–¾-in) border uncovered around the edge. Scatter over the garlic slices and oregano.

Cook in the middle of the preheated oven for 10–12 minutes or until crispy and golden. Remove from the oven and drizzle with a little more olive oil, season with sea salt and freshly ground black pepper and serve.

Marinara

Margherita

Unadulterated

This simple pizza is a great accompaniment to soup or salads. Pizza at its best!

Makes 1 pizza

1 x 30-cm (12-in) **Crispy pizza base (see page 28)**
125ml (4fl oz) **Quick classic tomato sauce (see page 170)**
75g (2¾oz) **mozzarella,** cubed
5–6 **basil leaves,** torn
Sea salt
1 Tbsp **extra virgin olive oil**

Prepare the pizza base so it is ready to be topped. Preheat the oven to 220°C/425°F/Gas mark 7. Spread the tomato sauce evenly over the base leaving a 1–2 cm (½–¾-in) border uncovered around the edge. Scatter over the mozzarella and torn basil leaves. Sprinkle over some salt and drizzle over the olive oil. Cook in the centre of the preheated oven for 10–12 minutes or until crispy and golden. Serve immediately.

Piccante

Spicy

This one is for Stuart West, our friend and photographer who helps make our books so enjoyable to do. He likes it spicy!

Makes 1 pizza

1 x 30-cm (12-in) **Crispy pizza base (see page 28)**
125ml (4fl oz) **Spicy tomato sauce (see page 168)**
100g (3½oz) **pepperoni slices**
8–12 **black olives,** stoned
50g (2oz) **grated Parmesan cheese**
Chilli oil, to serve

Preheat the oven to 220°C/425°F/Gas mark 7. Prepare the pizza base so it is ready to be topped.

Evenly spread the tomato sauce over the base leaving a 1–2-cm (½–¾-in) border uncovered around the edge. Place the pepperoni slices on top, scatter over the olives and sprinkle over the Parmesan. Cook in the middle of the preheated oven for 10–12 minutes or until crispy and golden. Drizzle with chilli oil when it comes out of the oven, if liked, and serve immediately.

Frutti di mare

Frutti di mare

Colourful

This pizza is covered with seafood. It takes a little longer to prepare, and probably a little longer to eat – but it's worth it!

Makes 1 pizza

1 x 30-cm (12-in) **Crispy pizza base (see page 128)**
125ml (4fl oz) **Spicy tomato sauce (see page 168)**
100g (3½oz) **small mussels,** in their shells and well rinsed
100g (3½oz) **clams,** in their shells and well rinsed
6–8 **whole raw prawns**
1 **clove garlic,** finely chopped
1 **handful flat-leaf parsley,** chopped
Sea salt and freshly ground black pepper
Extra virgin olive oil

Preheat the oven to 220°C/425°F/Gas mark 7. Prepare the pizza base so it is ready to be topped.

Bring a large pan of slightly salted water to the boil. Run the mussels and clams under cold running water and discard any that do not close when tapped sharply. Remove any beards and barnacles from the mussels. Quickly boil the mussels and clams in the water, for 1–2 minutes or until steamed open, then drain well. Discard any that do not open. Set aside to cool slightly.

Spread the tomato sauce evenly over the base leaving a 1–2-cm (½–¾-in) border uncovered around the edge. Scatter over the well-drained mussels and clams evenly and then add the prawns. Scatter over the garlic and half of the parsley and season well. Drizzle with oil and cook in the middle of the preheated oven for 10–12 minutes or until crispy and golden around the edges. Serve immediately, sprinkled with the remaining parsley.

Florentina

Oozing

If you are serving this pizza to egg lovers then you may want to add extra eggs and position them so that when cut into pieces each person gets a yolk. Just be careful, when you are cracking them on to the base, that they don't ooze everywhere!

Makes 1 pizza

1 x 30-cm (12-in) **Crispy pizza base (see page 28)**
125ml (4fl oz) **Quick classic tomato sauce (see page 170)**
1 **clove garlic,** thinly sliced
180g (6oz) **baby spinach leaves,** blanched and well drained
100g (3½oz) **mozzarella,** sliced
Grated fresh nutmeg
20g (1oz) **finely grated Parmesan cheese**
1 **spring onion,** finely sliced
2 **eggs**
Extra virgin olive oil
Freshly ground black pepper

Preheat the oven to 220°C/425°F/Gas mark 7. Prepare the pizza base so it is ready to be topped.

Evenly spread the tomato sauce over the base leaving a 1–2-cm (½–¾-in) border uncovered around the edge. Scatter the garlic, spinach and mozzarella over the sauce. Finely grate a little nutmeg all over the pizza and sprinkle on the Parmesan and spring onion. Cook in the middle of the preheated oven for 6 minutes then open the oven, pull out the rack and quickly crack the eggs on to the centre of the pizza. Return to the oven and cook for a further 4–6 minutes or until crispy and golden. Once cooked, drizzle with oil and a grind of black pepper then serve immediately.

Florentina

Quattro stagioni

Hearty

Quattro stagioni means "four seasons", and this pizza should be made with the toppings placed in four sections, representing each season. However, if you are sharing the pizza it makes more sense to distribute the ingredients around more evenly so everybody gets a little bit of everything.

Makes 1 pizza

1 x 30-cm (12-in) **Crispy pizza base (see page 28)**
75ml (2½fl oz) **Quick classic tomato sauce (see page 170)**
4 slices **Parma ham**
2 **tomatoes**, thinly sliced
50g (2oz) **small mushrooms**, thinly sliced
1 Tbsp **capers**, rinsed and drained
8–12 **black olives**, stoned
4–6 **anchovy fillets**
150g (5oz) **mozzarella**, sliced
Extra virgin olive oil

Prepare the pizza base so it is ready to be topped. Preheat the oven to 220°C/425°F/Gas mark 7.

Spread the tomato sauce evenly over the pizza base, leaving about 1–2cm (½–¾in) uncovered around the edge. Tear the Parma ham into strips and place over the sauce. Evenly scatter all the remaining ingredients (except the mozzarella and oil) over the ham and finally top with the sliced mozzarella.

Cook in the middle of the preheated oven for 10–12 minutes or until crisp and golden. Remove from the oven, drizzle with a little extra virgin olive oil and serve immediately.

Quattro formaggi

Rich

One of life's simple pleasures – bread served with cheese. Accompany this pizza with a good Chianti and I assure you you'll be happy!

Makes 1 pizza

1 x 30-cm (12-in) **Crispy pizza base (see page 28)**
75g (2¾oz) **ricotta**
50g (2oz) **mozzarella**, sliced
50g (2oz) **Gorgonzola**, sliced
30g (1¼oz) **Parmesan cheese**, finely grated
Freshly ground black pepper

Prepare the pizza base so it is ready to be topped. Preheat the oven to 220°C/425°F/Gas mark 7.

Put spoonfuls of ricotta here and there all over the pizza leaving a 1–2-cm (½–¾-in) border uncovered around the edge. Scatter over the mozzarella and Gorgonzola slices and finally, sprinkle over the Parmesan. Cook in the middle of the preheated oven for 10–12 minutes or until crispy and golden. Remove from the oven, season with black pepper and serve immediately.

■ *Sprinkle over a handful of basil leaves or rocket for a bit of colour just before serving.*

Funghi

Earthy

This is a classic pizza, where mushrooms are truly given the chance to shine. Speaking of mushrooms, don't feel obliged to stick to the ordinary variety. If your tomatoes lack lustre, follow the Tip below.

Makes 1 pizza

1 x 30-cm (12-in) **Crispy pizza base (see page 28)**
4–5 **mixed ripe tomatoes** (about 500g/1lb 2oz), blanched,
    peeled, deseeded and chopped (see Tip below)
⅛–¼ tsp **salt**
120g (4oz) **chestnut mushrooms**, finely chopped
10–15 **fresh oregano leaves**, roughly chopped
150g (5oz) **mozzarella**, sliced
Extra virgin olive oil, for drizzling
Salt and freshly ground black pepper

Prepare the pizza base so it is ready to be topped. Preheat the oven to 220°C/425°F/Gas mark 7.

Place the prepared tomatoes in a sieve and sprinkle with ⅛–¼ tsp salt. Allow to drain for 10 minutes, pushing firmly with the back of a spoon to release excess liquid. Spoon the tomatoes over the pizza base, leaving about 1–2cm (½–¾-in) uncovered around the edge. Top with mushrooms, oregano and slices of mozzarella. Finish with a drizzle of olive oil and salt and pepper to taste.

Cook in the middle of the preheated oven for 10–12 minutes, until the crust is golden and the cheese is bubbling. Serve immediately.

■ *If ripe tomatoes aren't available, use any of the tomato recipes featured in the Sauces chapter (see pages 162–171).*

Funghi

Capricciosa

Capricciosa

Macho

This classic concoction is the Italian version of the meat-lovers' pizza. To maintain classic status, be sure to use ripe tomatoes, fresh mozzarella, and the best charcuterie available.

Makes 1 pizza

1 x 30-cm (12-in) **Crispy pizza base (see page 28)**
350g (12oz) **mixed ripe tomatoes**
⅛ tsp **salt**
1 **clove garlic,** crushed
1 **small white onion,** thinly sliced
100g (3½oz) **chestnut mushrooms,** thinly sliced
50g (2oz) **pepperoni slices**
50g (2oz) **salami slices**
50g (2oz) **prosciutto slices**
50g (2oz) **black olives**
150g (5oz) **mozzarella,** sliced
Sea salt and freshly ground black pepper

Prepare the pizza base so it is ready to be topped. Preheat the oven to 220°C/425°F/Gas mark 7.

Roughly chop the tomatoes and place in a sieve over a bowl. Press the tomatoes firmly with the back of a spoon to release as much liquid as possible. Sprinkle with salt (and a pinch of sugar if the tomatoes aren't very sweet) and leave to drain for a further 10 minutes.

Spoon the tomatoes over the base, leaving about 1–2cm (½–¾in) uncovered around the edge, and sprinkle with crushed garlic. Top with the remaining ingredients and season with sea salt and pepper to taste. Bake for 10–12 minutes, or until the cheese has melted and the crust is golden. Serve immediately.

Puttanesca

Extra zing

A classic Italian pizza and sauce, curiously called *puttanesca*, or "in the whore's style". Perhaps the dark, briny, hot nature of the traditional ingredients – capers, anchovies, black olives and chillies – hint at the origin. Whatever the explanation, it makes for a very fine pizza.

Makes 1 pizza

1 x 30-cm (12-in) **Crispy pizza base (see page 28)**
½ quantity **Sweet cherry tomato sauce (see page 167)**
8 **anchovy fillets in oil,** drained
10 **kalamata olives**
2 Tbsp **capers**
1 tsp **finely chopped peperoncini (see Tip below)**
3 Tbsp **grated Parmesan cheese**
Extra virgin olive oil, for drizzling
2 Tbsp **roughly chopped flat-leaf parsley**

Prepare the pizza base so it is ready to be topped. Preheat the oven to 220°C/425°F/Gas mark 7.

Spoon the Sweet cherry tomato sauce over the pizza base leaving about 1–2cm (½–¾-in) uncovered around the edge. Top with anchovies, olives, capers, peperoncini and Parmesan. Cook in the middle of the preheated oven for 10–12 minutes, until crust is golden and cheese is bubbling. Remove from the oven and finish with a drizzle of olive oil and a sprinkling of parsley. Serve immediately.

■ *Peperoncini are small red, slightly sweet Italian chillies. If not available, use any type of red chilli.*

Puttanesca

Bianca

Bianca

Clean

A pure, (almost) perfectly white pizza, which the Italians aptly name *Bianca*. Such simple, clean flavours deserve the best ingredients. Reach for flaky sea salt, firm garlic and the freshest mozzarella you can find to do it full justice.

Makes 1 pizza

1 head **garlic**
1 x 30-cm (12-in) **Crispy pizza base (see page 28)**
2 Tbsp **olive oil**
150g (5oz) **mozzarella,** sliced
1 tsp **sea salt**
1 sprig **fresh rosemary,** needles removed and chopped

Preheat the oven to 220°C/425°F/Gas mark 7.

Wrap the whole head of garlic in foil and roast for 45 minutes, until soft. Cool slightly. Slice the top off the garlic head and squeeze the cloves into a bowl. Stir with a fork.

Prepare the pizza base so it is ready to be topped.

Brush the pizza base with 1 Tbsp olive oil. Distribute slices of mozzarella over the base, leaving about 1–2cm (½–¾-in) uncovered around the edge, then top with sea salt, garlic and chopped rosemary. Drizzle with the remaining olive oil.

Bake for 10–12 minutes, or until the cheese has melted and the crust is golden. Serve immediately.

Land and sea

Combining meat and seafood recipes in one chapter is a bold move. There are meat lovers, there are vegetarians, and there are vegetarians who dabble in seafood. Some meat lovers enjoy seafood. Some don't. Some vegetarians fish, but don't eat their catch. Others are firmly against the consumption of seafood, of any kind. And here you have land and sea pizzas, seemingly thrown together in one careless chapter.

But there's a catch. The land and sea do not join. You will not find surf and turf pizzas on the following pages, where meat and seafood are featured together on one confused pizza. No, we firmly believe land and sea are separate entities to be enjoyed exclusively on their own. Never the twain shall meet. Well, rarely.

Pizza is a perfect vehicle for fruits from the sea. The soft, chewy base is a waiting, seafood vessel. Pizza is also the perfect vehicle for meat. The elusive saltiness penetrates tomatoes, mingles with cheese and is punctuated by sea salt.

Land and sea. Enjoy them, one at a time.

Pissaladière

Classic

This is a speciality from Nice in southern France. It is actually an open tart but can be made with bread dough or pastry. We make it with pizza dough so, technically, in our minds, it becomes a pizza!

Makes 1 pizza

1 x 30-cm (12-in) **Thick-crust pizza base (see page 30)**
2 quantities **Caramelized onions (see page 171)**
75g (2¾oz) **anchovy fillets,** halved lengthways
About 20 **black olives,** stoned
1 tsp **fresh thyme leaves**
Extra virgin olive oil, to serve

Preheat the oven to 220°C/425°F/Gas mark 7. Roll the pizza base into a rectangular shape, about 30cm (12in) long and 20cm (8in) wide and leave to rest for about 10 minutes.

Evenly spread the Caramelized onions over the base leaving a 1–2-cm (½–¾-in) border uncovered around the edge. Arrange the anchovy fillets in a chequerboard pattern with rows about 4cm (1½in) apart and on the diagonal. Place an olive in the centre of each diamond and sprinkle over the thyme leaves. Cook in the middle of the preheated oven for 14–16 minutes or until crispy and golden and the base is cooked through. Remove from the oven, drizzle with extra virgin olive oil and serve hot or cold.

Pissaladière

Tomato salsa, salmon and caper

Tomato salsa, salmon and caper

Fresh

This pizza works really well on the barbecue. Just cook the base then add the toppings for a perfect summer meal or snack with a green salad on the side.

Makes 1 pizza

1 x 30-cm (12-in) **Crispy pizza base (see page 28)**
2 Tbsp **extra virgin olive oil**
2 Tbsp **capers,** rinsed, drained and roughly chopped
1 **clove garlic,** crushed
½ **red onion,** finely chopped
2 **tomatoes,** deseeded and finely chopped
Juice of ½ **lemon**
1 Tbsp **chopped fresh dill**
Sea salt and freshly ground black pepper
125g (4oz) **smoked salmon slices**
Crème fraîche, to serve (optional)

Prepare the pizza base so it is ready to be topped. Preheat the oven to 220°C/425°F/Gas mark 7.

Combine the olive oil, capers and garlic in a small bowl and brush over the whole pizza base. Cook in the middle of the preheated oven for 8–10 minutes or until crispy and golden.

While the base is cooking, prepare the salsa. Combine the red onion, chopped tomatoes, lemon juice and dill in a small bowl and season well. When the base is cooked remove it from the oven and lay the smoked salmon slices evenly over it leaving a 1–2-cm (½–¾-in) border uncovered around the edge. Scatter over the tomato salsa and serve immediately. Serve with a dollop of crème fraîche on each piece if liked.

All–day breakfast calzone

Wholesome

These are great after a big night out and are best served hot.

Makes 6 calzoni

1 **quantity Calzone dough**
(see page 30)
30–36 **Slow-roasted
tomatoes (see page 166)**
or sun-dried tomatoes
9–12 **sausages**
(about 600g/1lb 5oz)
300g (10oz) **mozzarella,
sliced**
6 slices **Parma ham**
6 **medium eggs**
Salt and freshly ground
black pepper
Extra virgin olive oil

Preheat the oven to
220°C/425°F/Gas mark 7.

Divide the dough into six
pieces. Put a piece of baking
parchment on a work
surface and roll out one ball
of dough into a 20-cm (8-in)
round. Reserve the remaining
balls in a bowl covered with
a clean tea towel. Evenly
place 5–6 tomatoes over
half of the round, leaving a
1-cm (½-in) border uncovered

around the edge. Squeeze
the sausagemeat from about
two casings into teaspoon-
sized balls. Top with 50g
(2oz) sliced mozzarella and
tear over one piece of Parma
ham. Make a small crater-
like hollow in the middle of
the assembled ingredients.
Crack 1 egg into the crater,
reserving a little of the egg
white, and season with salt
and pepper. Working quickly,
fold the uncovered side of
the round over the filling and
press the edges together to
seal them and form a
crescent shape. Brush with
egg white. Carefully transfer
to a baking sheet and bake
for 15 minutes, or until the
crust is golden and the
bottom of the calzone is
cooked through. Allow to
rest for a few minutes before
serving.

While the calzone is cooking,
continue preparing the
remaining calzoni. You can
make and cook more than
one calzone at a time if liked.

Duck, hoisin and spring onion
Oriental

We would always make this pizza using a thin crispy base so that it somewhat resembles the pancake that you would normally wrap your Peking duck in.

Makes 1 pizza

1 x 30-cm (12-in) **Crispy pizza base (see page 28)**
2 Tbsp **hoisin sauce**
2 **Peking duck legs,** cooked and meat shredded
2 **spring onions,** finely shredded
Extra virgin olive oil or chilli oil

Prepare the pizza base so it is ready to be topped. Preheat the oven to 220°C/425°F/Gas mark 7.

Spread the hoisin sauce evenly over the pizza base, leaving a 1-cm (½-in) border uncovered around the edge. Evenly scatter the duck and spring onions over the sauce and drizzle all over with a little oil. Cook in the middle of the preheated oven for 10–12 minutes or until crispy and golden. Serve immediately.

Walnut pesto and hot-smoked salmon

Walnut pesto and hot-smoked salmon

Indulgent

Lindsay's cousin's business, St Mary's River Smokehouses, produce the best hot-smoked salmon I have ever tasted. It is smoked using maple syrup, which imparts a succulent sweet flavour and also has a fantastic aroma.

Makes 1 pizza

1 x 30-cm (12-in) Crispy pizza base (see page 28)
2 Tbsp Walnut pesto (see page 164)
2 Tbsp crème fraîche
150g (5oz) hot-smoked salmon
1 small chicory, finely shredded (optional)
100g (3½oz) mozzarella, sliced
Salt and freshly ground black pepper
50g (2oz) watercress
Extra virgin olive oil

Prepare the pizza base so it ready to be topped. Preheat the oven to 220°C/425°F/Gas mark 7.

Combine the Walnut pesto and crème fraîche and spread evenly over the base, leaving about a 2-cm (¾-in) border uncovered around the edge. Scatter over the hot smoked salmon, chicory, if using, and mozzarella. Season generously with salt and freshly ground black pepper. Cook in the middle of the preheated oven for 10–12 minutes or until golden and crispy. Remove from the oven, sprinkle over the watercress, drizzle with extra virgin olive oil and serve immediately.

Prawn and rocket

Fragrant

The base for this pizza is topped with Slow-roasted tomato sauce (see page 167). The slow-roasting really intensifies the flavour of the tomatoes. Leave the little tails on the prawns for an authentic look.

Makes 1 pizza

1 x 30-cm (12-in) **Crispy pizza base (see page 28)**
½ quantity **Slow-roasted tomato sauce (see page 167)**
8–12 **peeled raw prawns,** tails left on
150g (5oz) **mozzarella,** sliced
Sea salt and freshly ground black pepper
50g (2oz) **rocket leaves**
Extra virgin olive oil or chilli oil

Prepare the pizza base so it is ready to be topped. Preheat the oven to 220°C/425°F/Gas mark 7.

Spread the Slow-roasted tomato sauce evenly over the pizza base, leaving about a 2-cm (¾-in) border uncovered around the edge. Evenly spread the prawns and sliced mozzarella over the sauce. Season with salt and pepper.

Cook in the middle of the preheated oven for 10–12 minutes or until crispy and golden. Remove from the oven, sprinkle over the rocket leaves, drizzle with oil and serve immediately.

Prawn and rocket

Pizza al tonno

Store-cupboard

Pizza with tinned tuna – you either love it or you hate it!
With the Spicy tomato sauce (see page 168) and salty capers
it really is a good pizza topping.

Makes 1 pizza

1 x 30-cm (12-in) **Crispy pizza base (see page 28)**
125ml (4fl oz) **Spicy tomato sauce (see page 168)**
160g (5½oz) **tinned tuna in oil,** drained
2 Tbsp **capers**
3 sprigs **fresh thyme,** leaves removed
100g (3½oz) **mozzarella,** sliced
Extra virgin olive oil, for drizzling
Basil leaves, torn, to serve

Prepare the pizza base so it is ready to be topped. Preheat the
oven to 220°C/425°F/Gas mark 7.

Spread the tomato sauce over the pizza base, leaving about a
2-cm (¾-in) border uncovered around the edge. Evenly spread the
tuna over the tomato sauce. Sprinkle over the capers and thyme
leaves and top with the mozzarella slices. Finally, drizzle with a little
extra virgin olive oil.

Cook in the middle of the preheated oven for 10–12 minutes or
until crispy and golden. Remove from the oven, drizzle with a little
more extra virgin olive oil and top with freshly torn basil leaves.
Serve immediately.

Spicy tomato, sausage and fennel seed
Fragrant

Sausagemeat on a pizza isn't always as crass as the offerings of your local pizza delivery company. Choose top-quality sausages and you will realize how good it can be!

Makes 1 pizza

1 x 30-cm (12-in) **Crispy pizza base (see page 28)**
125ml (4fl oz) **Spicy tomato sauce (see page 168)**
200g (7oz) **pork sausagemeat** (about 3 sausages)
1 **red pepper,** roasted, peeled and sliced
1 tsp **fennel seeds**
100g (3½oz) **mozzarella,** sliced
Extra virgin olive oil, for drizzling
1 small handful **basil leaves,** torn

Prepare the pizza base so it is ready to be topped. Preheat the oven to 220°C/425°F/Gas mark 7.

Spread the tomato sauce over the pizza base, leaving about 1–2cm (½–¾-in) uncovered around the edge. Evenly spread the sausagemeat, in about 1-tsp mounds, over the sauce. Top with the roasted pepper slices, fennel seeds and finally the mozzarella slices. Drizzle with a little olive oil.

Cook in the middle of the preheated oven for 10–12 minutes or until crispy and golden. Remove from the oven, drizzle with a little more extra virgin olive oil and top with freshly torn basil leaves. Serve immediately.

Red pepper sauce, chicken and olive
Simple

It's the sauce that really makes this pizza special. Try serving it with Basil pesto (see page 162).

Makes 1 pizza

1 large skinless chicken breast
1 x 30-cm (12-in) Crispy pizza base (see page 28)
125ml (4fl oz) Tomato and roasted red pepper sauce
  (see page 168)
100g (3½oz) mascarpone
Finely grated rind of 1 lemon
Freshly ground black pepper
1 tsp fresh thyme leaves
12 green olives
Extra virgin olive oil

Poach the chicken breast in a small pan of simmering water for 12–15 minutes or until cooked. Remove from the water and set aside to cool then slice into about 10–12 thin slices.

Prepare the pizza base so it is ready to be topped. Preheat the oven to 220°C/425°F/Gas mark 7.

Spread the Tomato and roasted red pepper sauce over the pizza base, leaving about a 1–2-cm (½–¾-in) border uncovered around the edge. Evenly place the chicken slices over the sauce. Combine the mascarpone, lemon rind, pepper and thyme in a small bowl, then place spoonfuls of this mixture evenly over the base. Top with the green olives and drizzle with a little extra virgin olive oil.

Cook in the middle of the preheated oven for 10–12 minutes or until crispy and golden. Remove from the oven, drizzle with the pesto, if using, or a little more olive oil and serve immediately.

Spinach, pancetta and ricotta

Rustic

We love using ricotta on pizzas because the nature of it means that it doesn't melt when cooked.

Makes 1 pizza

1 x 30-cm (12-in) **Crispy pizza base (see page 28)**
150g (5oz) **cubed pancetta**
125g (4oz) **ricotta cheese**
1 pinch **nutmeg**
3 **spring onions,** finely sliced
1 **egg**
Freshly ground black pepper
60ml (2½fl oz) **Quick classic tomato sauce (see page 170)**
200g (7oz) **fresh spinach,** washed, blanched and well drained
Extra virgin olive oil

Prepare the pizza base so it is ready to be topped. Preheat the oven to 220°C/425°F/Gas mark 7.

Heat a small non-stick frying pan and add the pancetta cubes. Cook for 3–4 minutes or until golden and crispy. Set aside on kitchen paper. Mix the ricotta cheese, nutmeg, half of the spring onions, egg and black pepper in a small bowl until just combined (do not beat the mixture). Spread the tomato sauce over the pizza base, leaving about a 1–2-cm (½–¾-in) border uncovered around the edge. Spoon the ricotta mixture randomly but evenly over the tomato. Top with the spinach leaves, pancetta and remaining spring onion slices.

Cook in the middle of the preheated oven for 10–12 minutes or until crispy and golden. Remove from the oven, drizzle with a little extra virgin olive oil and serve immediately.

Chicken, cranberry and brie

Sweet

Since this isn't such an authentic combination of pizza toppings we like to make it on our Thick-crust pizza base (see page 30). It becomes more like a large toasted sandwich and is good eaten hot or cold.

Makes 1 pizza

2 small chicken breasts
1 x 30-cm (12-in) Thick-crust pizza base (see page 30)
4 Tbsp shop-bought cranberry sauce
100g (3½oz) brie, sliced
4 Tbsp Caramelized onions (see page 171)
Freshly ground black pepper
Extra virgin olive oil

Put the chicken breasts in a pan of simmering water and poach for 10–12 minutes or until cooked through. Remove from the water and set aside to cool slightly (this can be done up to a day in advance).

Prepare the pizza base so it is ready to be topped. Preheat the oven to 220°C/425°F/Gas mark 7.

Spread the cranberry sauce evenly over the pizza base, leaving about a 1–2-cm (½–¾-in) border uncovered around the edge. Slice the chicken breasts and spread evenly over the sauce. Top with the brie slices, Caramelized onions and a good grind of black pepper.

Cook in the middle of the preheated oven for 14–16 minutes or until crispy and golden and the base is cooked. Remove from the oven, drizzle with a little extra virgin olive oil and serve immediately.

Chicken, cranberry and brie

Fennel relish and beef carpaccio

Fennel relish and beef carpaccio

Textural

Try this with Parma ham instead of bresaola if you prefer – it works well too!

Makes 1 pizza

1 x 30-cm (12-in) **Crispy pizza base (see page 28)**
1 quantity **Caramelized fennel relish (see page 169)**
150g (5oz) **mozzarella,** cubed
75g (2¾oz) **bresaola slices (about 8–10 slices)**
Handful **flat leaf parsley,** roughly chopped
Extra virgin olive oil, to serve

Prepare the pizza base so it is ready to be topped. Preheat the oven to 220°C/425°F/Gas mark 7.

Evenly spread the fennel relish over the base leaving a 1–2-cm (½–¾-in) border uncovered around the edge. Scatter over the mozzarella and cook in the middle of the preheated oven for 10–12 minutes or until crispy and golden. Remove from the oven and place the bresaola on the pizza, allowing about 1 piece per slice. Scatter over the parsley and drizzle with a little oil. Serve immediately.

Sweet chilli, shredded chicken and basil

Aromatic

If you can't get hold of Thai basil, which should be available from Oriental supermarkets, then just use regular basil. It still imparts a slightly aniseedy flavour and is also delicious with the chilli and chicken.

Makes 1 pizza

1 x 30-cm (12-in) **Crispy pizza base (see page 28)**
2–3 Tbsp **shop-bought sweet chilli sauce**
1 **small leek,** halved lengthways and finely sliced
5–6 **Thai basil leaves,** torn
2 **cooked chicken breasts,** shredded
Extra virgin olive oil or chilli oil

Prepare the pizza base so it is ready to be topped. Preheat the oven to 220°C/425°F/Gas mark 7.

Spread the sweet chilli sauce evenly over the base leaving about a 1–2-cm (½–¾-in) border uncovered around the edge. Scatter over the sliced leek and basil leaves then the chicken. Drizzle all over with extra virgin olive oil or chilli oil.

Cook in the middle of the preheated oven for 10–12 minutes or until crispy and golden. Remove from the oven and drizzle with a little more oil. Serve immediately.

Tomato, pumpkin, chorizo and spinach
Bold

This pizza is based on one of my favourite salads. The salad comes from Julie Le Clerc's *Simple Café Food* and, with the addition of chorizo and spinach, I think it makes a perfect pizza topping.

Makes 1 pizza

500g (1lb 2oz) **pumpkin,** peeled and cut into
   about 2-cm (¾-in) cubes
Extra virgin olive oil
1 x 30-cm (12-in) **Crispy pizza base (see page 28)**
3–4 Tbsp (about ½ quantity) **Sun-dried tomato pesto**
   (see page 165)
180g (6oz) **spinach,** blanched and well drained
100g (3½oz) **uncooked chorizo,** cut into small cubes
150g (5oz) **mozzarella,** sliced
Sea salt and freshly ground black pepper

Preheat the oven to 220°C/425°F/Gas mark 7.

Put the cubed pumpkin in a roasting dish and drizzle over 1 tsp olive oil. Toss to coat. Roast the pumpkin for 15–20 minutes or until cooked and golden. Set aside to cool slightly. Prepare the pizza base so it is ready to be topped.

Spread the Sun-dried tomato pesto evenly over the pizza base, leaving about a 1–2-cm (½–¾-in) border uncovered around the edge. Evenly spread the spinach, chorizo and pumpkin over the sauce. Top with the sliced mozzarella and season well. Cook in the middle of the preheated oven for 10–12 minutes or until crispy and golden. Remove from the oven, drizzle with a little extra virgin olive oil and serve immediately.

Wild mushroom, radicchio and bresaola

Wild mushroom, radicchio and bresaola

Autumnal

This rustic Italian pizza is a real autumn treat when wild mushrooms are in abundance.

Makes 1 pizza

1 x 30-cm (12-in) **Crispy pizza base** (see page 28)
1 Tbsp **extra virgin olive oil**
1 **clove garlic,** crushed
250g (9oz) **mixed wild mushrooms of choice**
1 **small radicchio,** roughly shredded
Freshly ground black pepper
150g (5oz) **soft goat's cheese**
3–4 **courgette flowers (optional)**
75g (2¾oz) **bresaola slices**
1 small bunch **flat-leaf parsley,** roughly chopped
Chilli oil, to serve

Prepare the pizza base so it is ready to be topped. Preheat the oven to 220°C/425°F/Gas mark 7.

Heat the olive oil in a frying pan over high heat. When the pan is very hot add the garlic, mushrooms and radicchio and sauté for 1–2 minutes or until the mushrooms are just wilted but not releasing liquid. Season generously with black pepper and set aside.

Spread the goat's cheese over the base leaving a 1–2-cm (½–¾-in) border, uncovered around the edge. Scatter over the mushrooms and radicchio and top with courgette flowers if using. Cook in the middle of the preheated oven for 10–12 minutes or until crispy and golden. Remove from the oven, top with the bresaola and parsley and drizzle with chilli oil. Serve immediately.

Calabrese, mushroom and cheese calzone

Hearty

Make sure you wait for a few minutes before tucking into these delicious calzoni – they'll be piping hot inside!

Makes 6 calzoni

1 quantity **Calzone dough** (see page 30)
1 quantity **Quick classic tomato sauce (page 170)**
100ml (3½fl oz) **Black olive tapénade (see page 169) (optional)**
175g (6oz) (24 thin slices) **calabrese salami**
180g (6½oz) **feta cheese, crumbled**
180g (6½oz) **chèvre**
300g (10oz) **block mozzarella,** grated
400g (14oz) **chestnut mushrooms,** thinly sliced
3 **ripe tomatoes,** each cut into 8 wedges

Preheat the oven to 220°C/425°F/Gas mark 7. Divide the pizza dough into six pieces. Put a piece of baking parchment on a work surface and roll out one ball of dough into a 20-cm (8-in) round. Reserve the remaining balls in a bowl covered with a clean tea towel.

Spoon 2 Tbsp tomato sauce and 1 Tbsp of the tapénade (if using) over the base. On one half of the round place 3–4 slices calabrese, 30g (1oz) feta, 30g (1oz) chèvre, 50g (2oz) mozzarella, a handful of mushroom slices and 4 tomato wedges. Fold the other half of the round over the filling and pinch the edges together to form a crescent shape.

Carefully transfer the baking parchment to a baking sheet and bake for 15 minutes or until crust is golden and the bottom of the calzone is cooked through. Allow to rest for a few minutes before serving. While the calzone is cooking, continue preparing the remaining calzoni. You can make and cook more than one calzone at a time if liked.

Calabrese, mushroom and cheese calzone

Coriander pesto, prawn and feta

Coriander pesto, prawn and feta

Fresh

Coriander pesto, packed with mint, garlic, chilli and walnuts, adds an incredible depth of flavour to tender prawns and salty feta cheese.

Makes 1 pizza

1 x 30-cm (12-in) **Crispy pizza base (see page 28)**
2 heaped Tbsp **Coriander pesto (see page 164)**
8–12 **raw prawns,** peeled **(see Tip below)**
75g (2¾oz) **feta cheese,** crumbled

Prepare the pizza base so it is ready to be topped. Preheat the oven to 220°C/425°F/Gas mark 7. Prepare the pesto and set aside.

Spoon the pesto over the pizza base leaving a 1–2-cm (½–¾-in) border, uncovered around the edge. Top with prawns, turning to coat in pesto. Finish with crumbled feta. Bake for 10–12 minutes until the crust is golden. Serve immediately.

■ *Cooked, frozen prawns can be substituted for fresh. Follow the recipe as above, except sauté the prawns to defrost and to remove excess moisture.*

Barbecued chicken

Substantial

A sweet, smoky, hearty pizza that is always a crowd pleaser.

Makes 1 pizza

1 x 30-cm (12-in) **Crispy pizza base (see page 28)**
1 quantity **Caramelized onions (see page 171)**
300g (10oz) **skinless chicken breasts**
1 Tbsp **olive oil**
100ml (3½fl oz) + 2 Tbsp **Mustard bourbon barbecue sauce**
   (see page 171 and Tip below)
200g (7oz) **Monterey Jack cheese**, grated
2 Tbsp **chopped coriander**

Prepare the pizza base so it is ready to be topped. Preheat the oven to 220°C/425°F/Gas mark 7.

Prepare the Caramelized onions and set aside. Cut the chicken breasts into bite-sized pieces. Heat the olive oil in a large frying pan over medium-high heat. Add the chicken and sauté until cooked through, about 6 minutes. Allow to cool slightly. In a large bowl toss the chicken with 2 Tbsp of the barbecue sauce, cover and refrigerate.

Spread 100ml (3½fl oz) of the barbecue sauce over the base leaving a 1–2-cm (½–¾-in) border uncovered around the edge. Top with Caramelized onions, chicken pieces, and finish with grated cheese. Bake for 10–12 minutes, until the crust is golden and the cheese is bubbling. Sprinkle with coriander and serve immediately.

■ *Our Mustard bourbon barbecue sauce (see page 171) is delicious but, if you are short of time, your favourite shop-bought barbecue sauce will make a fine alternative.*

Asiago, pancetta and chicory

Sophisticated

Pancetta lends a wonderful salty-smoky quality to this unique pizza.

Makes 1 pizza

1 x 30-cm (12-in) **Crispy pizza base (see page 28)**
1 Tbsp **olive oil**
150-g (5-oz) **piece pancetta,** cubed
5 **heads chicory,** chopped crossways and ends discarded
3 Tbsp **freshly grated Parmesan cheese**
Juice of ½ **lemon**
Sea salt and ground black pepper to taste
150g (5oz) **Asiago cheese,** grated

Prepare the pizza base so it is ready to be topped. Preheat the oven to 220°C/425°F/Gas mark 7.

Heat the olive oil in a large frying pan over medium-high heat. Add the pancetta and sauté until the edges begin to brown. Add the chicory and sauté, stirring occasionally, until it begins to wilt, about 5 minutes. Remove from the heat and stir in the Parmesan and lemon juice. Season with salt and pepper and set aside.

Spoon the chicory mixture over the base, leaving a 1–2-cm (½–¾-in) border uncovered around the edge, and cover with cheese. Bake for 10–12 minutes, until the crust is golden and cooked through in the centre. Remove from the oven, cool slightly and serve.

Caramelized onion, prosciutto and peach

Caramelized onion, prosciutto and peach

Summery

We first featured the wonderful combination of peaches and prosciutto in our last book, *Barbecue!* Here they are paired again, making sweet harmony on a pizza.

Makes 1 pizza

1 quantity **Caramelized onions (see page 171)**
1 x 30-cm (12-in) **Crispy pizza base (see page 28)**
8 pieces **thinly sliced prosciutto,** torn
2 **small peaches,** each cut into 8 wedges
75g (2¾oz) **chèvre,** crumbled
Freshly ground black pepper to taste

Prepare the Caramelized onions and set aside. Prepare the pizza base so it is ready to be topped. Preheat the oven to 220°C/425°F/Gas mark 7.

Spoon the onions over the base leaving a 1–2-cm (½–¾-in) border uncovered around the edge. Top with pieces of prosciutto and 12 peach wedges (eat the extras!). Finish with crumbled chèvre and ground pepper.

Bake for 10–12 minutes, until the crust is golden. Serve immediately.

Basil pesto, Genoa salami and mozzarella

Savoury

Here, simple flavours come together to create something far greater than the sum of their parts.

Makes 1 pizza

1 x 30-cm (12-in) **Crispy pizza base (see page 28)**
2 heaped Tbsp **Basil pesto (see page 162)**
150g (5oz) **mozzarella,** sliced
80g (3oz) **Genoa salami,** thinly sliced
Freshly ground black pepper
Basil leaves, to serve

Prepare the pizza base so it is ready to be topped. Preheat the oven to 220°C/425°F/Gas mark 7.

Spread the pesto over the base leaving a 1–2-cm (½–¾-in) border uncovered around the edge. Cover with mozzarella and top with salami. Finish with a twist of black pepper.

Bake for 10–12 minutes, or until the cheese has melted and the crust is golden. Serve immediately, topped with basil leaves.

Basil pesto, Genoa salami and mozzarella

Asparagus, bacon and cherry tomato

Asparagus, bacon and cherry tomato

Colourful

This colourful, spring-like pizza is best made with a thick crust. The asparagus and cherry tomatoes sink into the dough like a soft, chewy pillow.

Makes 1 pizza

1 x 30-cm (12-in) **Thick-crust pizza base (see page 30)**
5 **slices bacon,** chopped into 2-cm (¾-in) pieces or 50g (2oz)
   pancetta, cubed
200g (7oz) **mozzarella,** sliced
150g (5oz) **fresh asparagus,** woody stems removed, chopped
200g (7oz) **cherry tomatoes,** halved
50g (2oz) **goat's cheese,** crumbled
Freshly ground black pepper
Chilli oil

Prepare the pizza base so it is ready to be topped. Preheat the oven to 220°C/425°F/Gas mark 7.

Put the cubes of bacon in a large frying pan and set over medium-high heat. Cook until the fat is released and the bacon is just browned. Remove the bacon with a slotted spoon and drain on kitchen paper.

Place mozzarella slices over the base leaving a 1–2-cm (½–¾-in) border uncovered around the edge. Top with bacon slices, chopped asparagus and cherry tomatoes. Finish with crumbled goat's cheese and pepper to taste. Bake for 12–14 minutes, until the crust is golden and the base is cooked through in the centre. Remove from the oven, drizzle with chilli oil and serve immediately.

From the garden

Pippa and I are fine gardeners. We water our potted window herbs with care and attention. We lovingly snip leaves from pristine shop-bought basil plants. These are qualities one needs when creating garden-inspired pizzas. Each season brings bountiful produce. With the winter comes purple-sprouting broccoli and king cabbages. The spring welcomes asparagus, wild fennel and new potatoes. Baby greens, courgettes and corn mark the summer. Autumn is defined by pumpkins, wild mushrooms and Jerusalem artichokes.

All right. Pippa and I are urban gardeners. We carry baskets rather than spades. It's not our fault; there's concrete where soil should be. But our parents are good gardeners, and we paid attention. We understand seasonality and respect locally-grown produce. We coddle our fruits and vegetables. We water with care. And most of all, we're excellent weeders. One has to be when there are countless recipes that could have made their way into this delicious chapter. Once the results came in, we had to weed, and weed again. Gardening, after all, is hard work.

Jerusalem artichoke pizza bianca

Sophisticated

This white pizza is also delicious made on a Focaccia pizza base (see page 40). Try a drizzle of chilli oil just before serving if heat is your thing.

Makes 1 pizza

1 x 30-cm (12-in) **Crispy pizza base (see page 28)**
2 Tbsp **extra virgin olive oil**
2 Tbsp **capers,** roughly chopped
1 **clove garlic,** crushed
300g (10oz) **Jerusalem artichokes,** par-boiled for 5 minutes
   then sliced lengthways about 5mm (¼in) thick
100g (3½oz) **mozzarella,** sliced
Freshly ground black pepper
1–2 bunches **cherry tomatoes on the vine**

Prepare the pizza base so it is ready to be topped. Preheat the oven to 220°C/425°F/Gas mark 7.

Combine the olive oil, capers and garlic in a small bowl. Brush the oil mixture all over the base, using a pastry brush. Place the artichoke slices evenly over the base, leaving a 1–2-cm (½–¾in) border uncovered around the edge. Scatter over the mozzarella and a good grind of black pepper. Place the cherry tomatoes on top.

Cook in the middle of the preheated oven for 10–12 minutes or until crisp and golden. Serve immediately.

Jerusalem artichoke pizza bianca

Mushroom, rosemary and ricotta

Rustic

This pizza is quite rich so we like to serve it with a large green salad on the side.

Makes 1 pizza

1 x 30-cm (12-in) **Crispy pizza base (see page 28)**
30g (1oz) **dried porcini mushrooms,** soaked in warm water
Extra virgin olive oil
1 **onion,** finely chopped
1 tsp **finely chopped rosemary**
1 **clove garlic,** crushed
125g (4oz) **ricotta**
200g (7oz) **chestnut mushrooms,** sliced
100g (3½oz) **mozzarella,** sliced
50g (2oz) **rocket leaves**

Prepare the pizza base so it is ready to be topped. Preheat the oven to 220°C/425°F/Gas mark 7.

Drain the porcini mushrooms, squeezing out any excess water, and chop finely. Heat 1 Tbsp extra virgin olive oil in a non-stick frying pan and add the onion. Cook for 2–3 minutes or until translucent but not browned. Add the rosemary, garlic and chopped porcini and sauté for a further 2–3 minutes. Remove from the heat and cool slightly. Stir in the ricotta and spread the mixture evenly over the base leaving a 1–2-cm (½–¾in) border uncovered around the edge. Evenly scatter over the chestnut mushrooms and slices of mozzarella.

Cook in the middle of the preheated oven for about 10–12 minutes or until crisp and golden. Remove from the oven. Sprinkle over the rocket, drizzle with extra virgin olive oil and serve immediately.

Roasted vegetable and taleggio

Nourishing

This is a great pizza in which to use up any leftover roasted vegetables.

Makes 1 pizza

2 **courgettes,** halved lengthways and cut into chunks

1 **red or yellow pepper,** cut into 1.5-cm (⅝-in) cubes

1 **red onion,** peeled and cut into wedges

1 sprig **rosemary,** needles removed

1 tsp **extra virgin olive oil**

1 x 30-cm (12-in) **Crispy pizza base (see page 28)**

125ml (4fl oz) **Quick classic tomato sauce (see page 170)**

100g (3½oz) **taleggio cheese,** sliced

Salt and freshly ground black pepper

2 Tbsp **Parsley pesto (see page 163),** to serve (optional)

Prepare the roasted vegetables (this can be done up to 2 days in advance). Preheat the oven to 200°C/400°F/Gas mark 6. Put the courgettes, pepper, onion and rosemary in a roasting dish. Drizzle over the olive oil and toss to coat. Roast the vegetables for about 15–20 minutes or until cooked and golden. Set aside to cool slightly.

Prepare the pizza base so it is ready to be topped. Preheat the oven to 220°C/475°F/Gas mark 7.

Spread the tomato sauce over the base, leaving about a 1–2-cm (½–¾in) border uncovered around the edge. Evenly spread the vegetables over the sauce and top with the taleggio. Season well.

Cook in the middle of the preheated oven for 10–12 minutes or until crispy and golden. Remove from the oven, drizzle with the pesto (if using) and serve immediately.

Rocket and new potato focaccia

Nourishing

I once thought that potato and bread eaten together was far too heavy until I had this dish at Books for Cooks in London.

Makes 1 pizza

½ quantity **Focaccia pizza base dough (see page 40)**
4 Tbsp **Rocket pesto (see page 163)**
300g (10oz) **new potatoes,** par-boiled for 8–10 minutes then sliced lengthways, about 5mm (¼in) thick
40g (1½oz) **grated Gruyère cheese**
Sea salt and freshly ground black pepper
50g (2oz) **rocket leaves**
Chilli oil, to serve

On a lightly floured work surface roll out the dough into a rectangular shape about 30cm (12in) long and 20cm (8in) wide. Place on baking parchment or a baking sheet ready to be topped and leave to rest for 15–20 minutes. Preheat the oven to 220°C/425°F/Gas mark 7.

Make small indentations on the top of the dough using your fingertips. Spread the rocket pesto evenly over the base, leaving about a 1–2-cm (½–¾in) border around the edges. Evenly place the potatoes over the pesto so they slightly overlap. Sprinkle over the Gruyère and season with salt and pepper. Cook in the middle of the preheated oven for about 14–16 minutes or until crisp and golden and the base is cooked through. Remove from the oven and throw over some fresh rocket leaves and a drizzle of chilli oil to serve.

Rocket and new potato focaccia

Roasted red onion, artichoke and sage

Roasted red onion, artichoke and sage

Simplicity

London's Portobello Road market on a Saturday morning is a great place to pick up a quick and tasty snack. I had a pizza very similar to this from The Grocer on Elgin, which is a gourmet deli just off Portobello Road.

Makes 2 long pizzas

2 **red onions,** peeled and cut into thin wedges
200g (7oz) **marinated artichokes,** drained and quartered
12–16 **sage leaves**
1 tsp **extra virgin olive oil**
¼ quantity **Crispy pizza base dough (see page 28)**
100ml (3½fl oz) **Quick classic tomato sauce (see page 170)**
30g (1¼oz) **finely grated Parmesan cheese**
Chilli oil, to serve

Preheat the oven to 220°C/425°F/Gas mark 7. Put the onion, artichokes and sage leaves in a roasting tray with 1 tsp extra virgin olive oil. Cook for 15–20 minutes or until golden and starting to go crispy.

Divide the pizza dough into two balls. On a lightly floured surface roll each ball into an oblong shape about 25cm (10in) long and 10cm (4in) wide. Transfer the bases to a baking sheet ready to be topped and leave to rest.

Spread the tomato sauce evenly over the bases, leaving about a 1-cm (½-in) border around the edge. Evenly scatter over the red onion wedges, artichoke quarters, sage leaves and Parmesan. Cook in the middle of the preheated oven for 10–12 minutes or until golden and crispy. Serve immediately with chilli oil drizzled over.

Grilled courgette, mint and goat's cheese

Springtime

We love the combination of mint and courgettes. For a non-vegetarian version tear over a few slices of Parma ham just before serving.

Makes 1 pizza

1 x 30-cm (12-in) **Crispy pizza base (see page 28)**
2 **medium courgettes,** sliced lengthways about 3–4 mm (⅛–¼in) thick **(see Tip below)**
1 Tbsp **extra virgin olive oil**
1 **clove garlic,** crushed
6–8 **mint leaves,** finely sliced, plus extra to serve
Sea salt and freshly ground black pepper
½ quantity **Sweet cherry tomato sauce (see page 167)**
100g (3½oz) **goat's cheese**

Prepare the pizza base so it is ready to be topped. Preheat the oven to 220°C/425°F/Gas mark 7.

Heat a grill pan to very hot and grill the courgette slices for 2–3 minutes on the first side and 1–2 minutes on the second side or until cooked through. Remove from the heat and combine with the oil, garlic and sliced mint leaves. Season well and set aside.

Evenly spread the tomato sauce over the base, leaving a 1–2-cm (½–¾in) border around the edge. Scatter over the courgette slices and crumble over the goat's cheese. Cook in the middle of the preheated oven for 10–12 minutes or until crispy and golden. Remove from the oven and scatter over a few extra mint leaves and serve immediately.

■ *Use a combination of green and yellow courgettes, if they are available, for an impressive look.*

Cherry tomato, leek and Gorgonzola
Substantial

Our Sweet cherry tomato sauce is made using a little honey, which goes particularly well with the Gorgonzola.

Makes 1 pizza

1 x 25-cm (10-in) **Focaccia pizza base (see page 40)**
½ quantity **Sweet cherry tomato sauce (see page 167)**
1 **medium leek,** trimmed, halved and finely sliced
   (about 90g/3¼oz)
100g (3½oz) **Gorgonzola cheese,** cubed
Freshly ground black pepper
Extra virgin olive oil
4–6 **basil leaves**

Prepare the pizza base so it is ready to be topped. Preheat the oven to 220°C/425°F/Gas mark 7.

Spread the Sweet cherry tomato sauce evenly over the base, leaving a 1–2-cm (½–¾in) border around the edge. Evenly spread the chopped leek and Gorgonzola over the sauce and grind over some black pepper. Finally drizzle with a little extra virgin olive oil.

Cook in the middle of the preheated oven for 14–16 minutes or until crispy and golden and the base is cooked through. Remove from the oven and drizzle with a little more extra virgin olive oil. Scatter over the basil leaves and serve immediately.

Red pepper and aubergine calzone

Hearty

The cheese oozes out when these calzoni are cut so it is best to let them rest for a few minutes before tucking in.

Makes 6 calzoni

Extra virgin olive oil
3 **medium aubergines,** cut into 1-cm (½in) cubes
Salt and freshly ground black pepper
1 quantity **Calzone dough (see page 30)**
300ml (10fl oz) **Tomato and roasted red pepper sauce (see page 168)**
300g (10oz) **mozzarella,** sliced
150g (5oz) **grated Parmesan cheese**
1 **handful basil leaves,** torn

Heat 2–3 tsp olive oil in a large non-stick frying pan and sauté the aubergine cubes until golden and cooked. Season to taste and set aside to cool slightly. Preheat the oven to 220°C/425°F/Gas mark 7.

Divide the dough into six pieces. Put a piece of baking parchment on a work surface and roll out one ball of dough into a 20-cm (8-in) round. Reserve the remaining dough balls in a bowl covered with a clean tea towel.

Spread about 3–4 Tbsp of the sauce over one half of the base, leaving 2cm (1in) as a rim. Evenly spread over one sixth of the aubergines and top with 50g (2oz) mozzarella, 25g (1oz) Parmesan and a few basil leaves. Fold the uncovered half of the dough over the filling and, using your fingers, crimp the edge to seal it forming a crescent shape.

Transfer the parchment to a baking sheet and bake for 15 minutes, or until the crust is golden and the bottom of the calzone is cooked. Rest for a few minutes before serving. While the calzone is cooking, prepare the remaining calzoni. Make and cook more than one calzone at the same time if liked.

Salsa verde and artichoke

Green

This pizza is full of flavour and packed with goodness.

Makes 1 pizza

1 x 30-cm (12-in) **Crispy pizza base (see page 28)**
3–4 **anchovy fillets**
2 Tbsp **capers,** rinsed
1 small bunch **flat-leaf parsley** (about 5g/⅛oz)
1 **clove garlic**
150g (5oz) **artichoke hearts,** drained and quartered
100g (3½oz) **mozzarella,** sliced
50g (2oz) **rocket leaves**
Freshly ground black pepper
Extra virgin olive oil

Prepare the pizza base so it is ready to be topped. Preheat the oven to 220°C/425°F/Gas mark 7.

To make the salsa verde, use a large, sharp knife and roughly chop the anchovy fillets, capers, parsley and garlic. Combine to form a coarse paste. Spread the salsa verde over the base, leaving a 1–2-cm (½–¾in) border around the edge, and top with the artichoke quarters. Top with the mozzarella slices.

Cook in the middle of the preheated oven for 10–12 minutes or until golden and crispy. Remove from the oven and top with the rocket leaves and a good grind of fresh black pepper. Drizzle over a little extra virgin olive oil and serve immediately.

Pear, Gouda and cumin

Pear, Gouda and cumin

Intriguing

This unique combination creates a gently sweet, tart, yet pungent pizza. The light, simple toppings make a perfect accompaniment to a soup or salad.

Makes 1 pizza

1 x 30-cm (12-in) **Crispy pizza base (see page 28)**
250g (9oz) **Gouda cheese,** grated
1 **large Bosc pear (see Tip below)**
½ tsp **cumin seeds**
1 Tbsp **pine nuts,** toasted
Extra virgin olive oil, for drizzling
Sea salt to taste
Basil leaves, to serve

Prepare the pizza base so it is ready to be topped. Preheat the oven to 220°C/425°F/Gas mark 7.

Sprinkle the Gouda evenly over the base leaving a 1–2-cm (½–¾in) border around the edge. Slice the pear into thin slices from top to bottom around the core. Discard the core. Distribute the pear slices over the cheese and sprinkle with cumin seeds and pine nuts. Drizzle with olive oil and a sprinkling of sea salt. Bake until the cheese has melted and the crust is golden. Serve immediately, topped with torn basil leaves.

■ *Bosc pears are large, slender pears with rust-coloured skin that hold their shape well when baked. Any pear, however, will do. Increase the quantity if the pears are small.*

Tomato, sweet potato and red onion

Caramelized

A pizza stone, which creates a very hot, professional environment in the oven, is useful for this pizza. The lush, colourful ingredients are piled so high that extra heat is helpful.

Makes 1 pizza

2 **large red onions**
2 Tbsp **olive oil**
1 tsp **caster sugar**
Salt and pepper
350g (12oz) **mixed ripe tomatoes**
1 x 30-cm (12-in) **Crispy pizza base (see page 28)**
1 **small sweet potato, peeled and thinly sliced**
1 **sprig fresh rosemary, needles removed and chopped**
250g (9oz) **taleggio cheese, cut into 1-cm (½-in) cubes**

Preheat the oven to 220°C/425°F/Gas mark 7.

Peel the onions and cut each onion into 8 wedges. Place in a roasting tin and toss with olive oil, sugar, and season with salt and pepper to taste. Roast the onions for 30 minutes, stirring every 10 minutes, until slightly charred and caramelized. Remove from the heat.

Roughly chop the tomatoes and place in a sieve over a bowl. Press the tomatoes with the back of a spoon to release as much liquid as possible. Sprinkle with ⅛ tsp salt (and a pinch of sugar if the tomatoes aren't very sweet) and leave to drain for a further 10 minutes.

Prepare the pizza base so it is ready to be topped. Spoon the tomatoes evenly over the base leaving a 1–2-cm (½–¾in) border around the edge. Top with red onions, sweet potato, rosemary and cheese. Bake for 12–15 minutes until the crust is golden and the centre is cooked through. Cool slightly, then slice and serve with forks and knives – toppings need taming with this pizza!

Mango salsa, pesto and goat's cheese

Fusion

Colours and flavours abound in this hot, sour, and salty-sweet pizza.

Makes 1 pizza

1 x 30-cm (12-in) **Crispy pizza base (see page 28)**
2 heaped Tbsp **Coriander pesto (see page 164)**
100g (3½oz) **goat's cheese,** crumbled

For the mango salsa:
1 **mango,** peeled, stone removed and the flesh finely cubed
1 **small red pepper,** cored and finely cubed
120g (4oz) **red onion,** finely chopped
20g (¾oz) **fresh coriander,** finely chopped
1 **red chilli,** deseeded and finely chopped
50ml (2fl oz) **sweet chilli sauce**
Juice of 1 **lime**

Prepare the pizza base so it is ready to be topped. Preheat the oven to 220°C/425°F/Gas mark 7.

Spread the base with Coriander pesto. Place the salsa ingredients in a small bowl and stir to combine. Spoon half of the salsa over the base, leaving a 1–2-cm (½–¾in) border around the edge, and reserve the rest for use in another recipe. (It is excellent with tortilla or pitta crisps, and will keep in the fridge for 24 hours). Top with the crumbled goat's cheese.

Bake for 10–12 minutes, until the crust is golden and cooked through in the centre. Serve immediately.

Tomato, chicory and blue cheese

Distinctive

This simple, juicy pizza is filled with layers of intriguing flavours and textures.

Makes 1 pizza

1 x 30-cm (12-in) **Crispy pizza base (see page 28)**
½ quantity **Sweet cherry tomato sauce (see page 167)**
1 Tbsp **olive oil**
4 **heads chicory,** finely sliced, ends discarded
50g (2oz) **radicchio,** finely sliced
Sea salt and ground black pepper
150g (5oz) **cambozola or any creamy blue cheese,**
  roughly sliced

Prepare the pizza base so it is ready to be topped. Preheat the oven to 220°C/425°F/Gas mark 7. Prepare the Sweet cherry tomato sauce and set aside.

Heat the olive oil in a heavy-bottomed frying pan over medium-high heat. Add the sliced chicory and radicchio and sauté, stirring occasionally, until wilted and slightly translucent, about 5 minutes. Season with sea salt and ground black pepper. Spoon the cherry tomato sauce over the base leaving a 1–2-cm (½–¾in) border around the edge. Add the sautéed chicory and radicchio and finish with slices of cambozola.

Bake in the middle of the oven for 10–12 minutes or until the crust is golden. Remove from the oven and allow to rest for 1–2 minutes. Slice and serve immediately.

Tomato, chicory and blue cheese

Wild mushroom, havarti and spinach

Wild mushroom, havarti and spinach
Seasonal

This woodsy, flavoursome pizza, filled with vitamin-rich spinach and the essential vitamins and minerals of mushrooms, will simultaneously satiate and enrich the body. That's a lot for one little pizza.

Makes 1 pizza

1 x 30-cm (12-in) Crispy pizza base (see page 28)
1 Tbsp olive oil
2 cloves garlic, finely chopped
200g (7oz) mixed wild mushrooms
150g (5oz) fresh spinach, trimmed and washed
¼ tsp sea salt
⅛ tsp freshly ground black pepper
2 Tbsp Basil pesto (see page 162)
4–5 sage leaves, finely chopped
250g (9oz) havarti cheese, cut into 1-cm (½-in) cubes

Prepare the pizza base so it is ready to be topped. Preheat the oven to 220°C/425°F/Gas mark 7.

Heat the olive oil in a frying pan and add the garlic and mushrooms. Sauté for 2–3 minutes, stirring regularly, until the garlic is fragrant and the mushrooms are coated. Add the spinach and stir, occasionally, until wilted. Sprinkle with sea salt and pepper and remove the pan from the heat.

Spread the pesto evenly over the base leaving a 1–2-cm (½–¾in) border around the edge. Top with the mushroom and spinach mixture, sage leaves and cubed havarti. Bake for 12–15 minutes, until the cheese and crust are golden. Serve immediately.

Rainbow chard, garlic and feta

Electric

Rainbow chard is a beautiful spring green with stalks ranging in colour from pale green, to gold, to bright red. Its cousin, Swiss chard, makes a perfectly suitable alternative.

Makes 1 pizza

1 x 30-cm (12-in) **Crispy pizza base (see page 28)** or 1 **Thick-crust pizza base (see page 30)**
1 bunch (about 500g/1lb 2oz) **rainbow chard,** ribs discarded
2 Tbsp **olive oil**
2 **cloves garlic,** crushed
Sea salt and ground black pepper
200g (7oz) **block mozzarella,** grated
100g (3½oz) **feta cheese,** crumbled
1 Tbsp **chilli oil**

Prepare the pizza base so it is ready to be topped. Preheat the oven to 220°C/425°F/Gas mark 7.

Bring a large pan of salted water to the boil. Add the chard and cook just until tender, about 2 minutes. Drain, rinse with cold water, drain again and squeeze out excess water. Transfer the chard to a chopping board and roughly chop. Heat the olive oil in a large frying pan and add the garlic. Sauté until fragrant, about 30 seconds, then add the chopped chard. Sauté for a further minute, then season with salt and pepper to taste.

Cover the base with mozzarella, leaving a 1–2-cm (½–¾in) border around the edge, then the cooked chard. Top with feta and drizzle with chilli oil. Bake for 10–12 minutes for the thin base, 12–14 minutes for the thick base, until the crust is golden and cooked through in the centre. Serve immediately.

Grilled pizza with red onion and pesto
Toothsome

Grilling pizza is pure bliss, as long as you follow three basic rules: 1 – use our Grilled pizza base dough recipe. It's soft, yet dense enough to keep its shape on the grill. 2 – accept this will be a casual, eat-when-it's-ready, meal. 3 – the topping we've given is just a suggestion. Experiment with whatever ingredients you have to hand. This pizza can only be cooked on a barbecue with a lid.

Makes 6 pizzas

1 quantity **Coriander pesto (see page 164)**
6 x 20-cm (8-in) **Grilled pizza bases (see page 35)**
Extra virgin olive oil, for brushing
1 **red onion,** thinly sliced
150g (5oz) **goat's cheese,** sliced

Prepare the pesto and set aside.

Preheat the barbecue to high on one side, warm on the other. Brush one side of a round of dough with olive oil. Pick up the dough with both hands and place, oiled-side down, on the hot side of the barbecue. Grill until grill marks appear, 2–3 minutes. Flip the dough and arrange the pesto, onions and 25g (1oz) goat's cheese on the cooked side. When the bottom has browned, slide the pizza to the cooler side of the barbecue. Close the lid and grill the pizza until the toppings are hot, and the cheese has melted. Transfer the pizza to a chopping board, and continue with the next round of dough. Cut the pizzas and serve immediately.

Sweet potato, sage and cambozola
Unique

I sampled this unique combination many years ago at an Italian restaurant in Halifax, Nova Scotia, and have been inspired by it ever since. Ultra-thin sweet potatoes can be achieved with a sharp knife, or better still, a mandolin cutter.

Makes 1 pizza

1 x 30-cm (12-in) **Crispy pizza base (see page 28)**
1 tsp **chilli oil**
150g (5oz) **cambozola cheese,** roughly sliced
175g (6oz) **sweet potato,** peeled and thinly sliced
4–5 **fresh sage leaves,** thinly sliced
Sea salt and freshly ground pepper

Prepare the pizza base so it is ready to be topped. Preheat the oven to 220°C/425°F/Gas mark 7.

Spread the base with chilli oil leaving a 1–2-cm (½–¾in) border around the edge. Top with cambozola then the slices of sweet potato. Scatter with sage leaves and season with salt and pepper.

Bake for 10–12 minutes until the crust is golden and the sweet potatoes are cooked through. Serve immediately.

Sweet potato, sage and cambozola

Ricotta, pesto, courgette and Parmesan

Ricotta, pesto, courgette and Parmesan

Creamy

Combining ricotta with basil pesto creates a creamy, rich base to any pizza. Here we've paired it with colourful courgettes, fresh from the garden.

Makes 1 pizza

1 x 30-cm (12-in) **Crispy pizza base (see page 28)**
150g (5oz) **ricotta**
3 Tbsp **Basil pesto (see page 162)**
2 **small courgettes,** thinly sliced (see Tip below)
20g (¾oz) **Parmesan cheese,** grated
Sea salt and pepper
1 small handful **fresh parsley leaves,** torn

Prepare the pizza base so it is ready to be topped. Preheat the oven to 220°C/425°F/Gas mark 7.

Combine the ricotta and pesto in a small bowl. Spread evenly over the base, leaving a 1–2-cm (½–¾in) border around the edge, and top with sliced courgette. Sprinkle over the grated Parmesan.

Bake for 10–12 minutes, until the crust is golden and the courgettes are slightly curled. Season with sea salt and pepper, and cover with torn parsley leaves. Serve immediately.

■ *Use a combination of yellow and green courgettes if available.*

Gorgonzola and roasted red onion

Sophisticated

Blue cheese, of any kind, elevates pizza to a grown-up level. Any blue will do, but we do love a good Gorgonzola.

Makes 1 pizza

2 large red onions
2 Tbsp olive oil
2 tsp caster sugar
Salt and pepper
1 x 30-cm (12-in) Crispy pizza base (see page 28)
250g (9oz) Gorgonzola cheese, crumbled
1 handful fresh flat-leaf parsley, torn

Preheat the oven to 220°C/425°F/Gas mark 7.

Peel the onions and cut each one into 8 wedges. Place them in a roasting tin and toss with olive oil, sugar and season with salt and pepper. Roast the onions for 30–40 minutes, stirring every 10 minutes, until caramelized. Remove from the heat and leave the oven on at the same temperature.

Prepare the pizza base so it is ready to be topped. Top the base with Gorgonzola and roasted red onions leaving a 1–2-cm (½–¾in) border around the edge. Bake for 10–12 minutes, or until the cheese has melted and the crust is golden. Sprinkle with parsley and serve immediately.

Gorgonzola and roasted red onion

Tomato pesto, Asiago and spinach

Tomato pesto, Asiago and spinach

Fresh

Is it a salad or a pizza? We like to think it's a lovely combination of both.

Makes 1 pizza

1 x 30-cm (12-in) **Crispy pizza base (see page 28)**
100ml (3½fl oz) **Sun-dried tomato pesto (see page 165)**
250g (9oz) **Asiago cheese,** grated
2 tsp **extra virgin olive oil**
1 tsp **balsamic vinegar**
1 tsp **maple syrup or honey**
Sea salt
200g (7oz) **baby spinach,** washed and dried (see Tip below)

Prepare the pizza base so it is ready to be topped. Preheat the oven to 220°C/425°F/Gas mark 7.

Spread the pesto evenly over base leaving a 1–2-cm (½–¾in) border around the edge. Top with Asiago cheese and bake for 10 minutes, until the crust is golden.

Combine the olive oil, balsamic vinegar, maple syrup and salt to taste. Toss with the spinach and mound over the pizza. Serve immediately.

■ *Substitute rocket, watercress or other greens for the baby spinach.*

Walnut pesto, aubergine and pomegranate

Intriguing

Roasted aubergine, tossed in an intriguing pomegranate molasses vinaigrette, spooned over walnut pesto and finished with glistening pomegranate seeds, makes for an intensely flavoured, divine pizza.

Makes 1 pizza

1 x 30-cm (12-in) **Crispy pizza base (see page 28)**
3 Tbsp **Walnut pesto (see page 164)**
350g (12oz) **aubergine,** cut into 2-cm (¾-in) cubes
2 Tbsp **extra virgin olive oil**
60g (2¼oz) **crumbled feta cheese**
2 Tbsp **pomegranate seeds**

For the vinaigrette:
2 Tbsp **olive oil**
1 Tbsp **pomegranate molasses**
1 tsp **runny honey**
¼ tsp **cumin seeds,** lightly crushed

Prepare the pizza base so it is ready to be topped. Preheat the oven to 220°C/425°F/Gas mark 7.

Prepare the Walnut pesto and set aside. Put the aubergine cubes in a roasting pan and toss with olive oil. Roast for 20 minutes, until slightly wilted and discoloured. Remove from the heat and keep the oven on at the same temperature. Toss the vinaigrette ingredients in a medium-sized bowl and add the roasted aubergine cubes, tossing to coat.

Spread the Walnut pesto over the base leaving a 1–2-cm (½–¾in) border around the edge. Spoon the aubergine cubes over the pesto and top with feta. Bake in the middle of the oven for 10–12 minutes, until the crust is golden. Remove from the oven, garnish with pomegranate seeds and serve immediately.

Walnut pesto, aubergine and pomegranate

Kids

My childhood Fridays were defined by pizzas. That was when two big pizza pans came out of the cupboard, dough was rolled, sauce was simmered, someone grated the cheese, someone else sliced the toppings and into the oven they went. Then the scissors were drawn. Scissors? Yes, the craziest, longest spears of metal a person has ever seen. One quick snip could cut a whole pizza in half.

Friday night pizza at the Camerons isn't an original idea. There are many families out there who reserve Friday night for this familial ritual. It's no wonder – pizzas can be created, one at a time, to suit the picky, sensitive tastebuds of every family member.

Take my sister Lee, for example. By hanging on to the apron strings, Lee could steer and shape her pizza the way she liked it – a huge deal in a family of four daughters. Lee brought Friday night pizzas to university, where she introduced the ritual to her flatmates. Then, one day, after global travels and many slices of pizza, the moon hit her eye like a big pizza pie – she fell in love with a man whose Friday nights were also devoted to pizza. He even made his own dough.

Sausage and spinach pizza

Comforting

This is a healthy favourite for kids. Sneak in a whole lot of extra goodness by using our Hidden vegetable tomato sauce for kids (see page 170).

Makes 1 pizza

1 x 30-cm (12-in) **Crispy pizza base (see page 28)**
125ml (4fl oz) **Hidden vegetable tomato sauce for kids**
  (see page 170)
2–3 **sausages of choice** (about 200g/7oz)
200g (7oz) **baby spinach leaves,** blanched and well drained
150g (5oz) **mozzarella,** sliced

Prepare the pizza base so it is ready to be topped. Preheat the oven to 220°C/425°F/Gas mark 7.

Evenly spread the sauce over the base, leaving a 1–2-cm (½–¾-in) border around the edge. Squeeze the sausagemeat from the casings and evenly scatter over the sauce in small teaspoon-sized amounts. Scatter over the cooked spinach leaves and mozzarella slices.

Cook in the middle of the preheated oven for 10–12 minutes or until crispy and golden. Serve immediately.

Bacon and egg pizza pie

Substantial

This scone-based pizza is more like a bacon and egg pie than a pizza – but then "pizza" literally means "pie" anyway!

Makes 1 pizza

1 x 25-cm (10-in) **Quick scone base (see page 29)**
2 **thin slices bacon,** chopped into small cubes
30g (1oz) **grated Cheddar cheese (optional)**
2 **eggs,** beaten
1 **spring onion,** finely sliced
1 tsp **milk**
Salt and freshly ground black pepper

Prepare the Quick scone base by pinching up the edges to form a rim about 1cm (½in) high. Preheat the oven to 200°C/400°F/Gas mark 6.

Evenly scatter the bacon over the base. If using the cheese scatter it over the bacon at this point. Beat the eggs, spring onion and milk together in a small jug and season well with salt and pepper. Pour the egg mixture over the bacon, ensuring it does not spill over the rim.

Put straight into the preheated oven and cook for 12–16 minutes or until the egg has set and the base is cooked. Serve warm or cold.

Quick ham, courgette and Cheddar
Simplicity

This is a great pizza for the kids to get involved in. It requires no rising so can go from hand to mouth in 30 minutes! Grating the courgettes will help disguise them and put any vegetable-hater off the scent.

Makes 1 pizza

1 x 25-cm (10-in) **Quick scone base (see page 29)**
60ml (2fl oz) **Quick classic tomato sauce (see page 170)**
1 **courgette,** grated
3 **slices ham,** chopped into cubes
50g (2oz) **grated Cheddar cheese**

Prepare the Quick scone base so it is ready to be topped. Preheat the oven to 200°C/400°F/Gas mark 6.

Spread the tomato sauce evenly over the base, leaving a 1cm (½in) border around the edge. Evenly scatter the courgette and ham over the sauce and sprinkle over the grated cheese.

Cook in the middle of the preheated oven for 12–16 minutes or until golden and cooked. Remove from the oven and allow to cool slightly before serving.

Quick ham, courgette and Cheddar

Pizza fingers

Pizza fingers

Fun

These are like a thickened version of Pizza breads (see page 39) and make a great snack for kids, and adults too!

Makes about 12 fingers

½ quantity **Focaccia pizza base dough (see page 40)**
Extra virgin olive oil (optional)

Suggested toppings
- 50g (2oz) **pepperoni,** finely sliced, 30g (1oz) **Gruyère cheese** and 1 tsp **dried oregano**
- Brush with 1 Tbsp **Pesto (see pages 162–165) combined** with 1 Tbsp **olive oil and top with** 30g (1oz) **Gruyère cheese**
- Brush with 1 Tbsp **chilli oil and top with** 30g (1oz) **finely grated Gruyère cheese and** 1 tsp **thyme leaves**
- Spread with 2 Tbsp **Quick classic tomato sauce (see page 170) and top with** 30g (1oz) **grated Cheddar cheese**
- Brush with 1 Tbsp **basil oil and sprinkle over sea salt**
- Brush with 2 Tbsp **melted butter and chopped herbs of your choice**

Preheat the oven to 220°C/425°F/Gas mark 7. Prepare the Focaccia pizza base dough so it is ready to be shaped. Shape the dough into ovals about 30cm (12in) long and 20cm (8in) wide and place on a lightly floured baking sheet. Make cuts right through the dough, about 2cm (1in) apart, but so they are still attached at the ends, and leave to rest, covered, for 10–15 minutes.

Cover the surface of the dough with your selected toppings and cook for 14–16 minutes or until golden and crispy. Serve straight from the oven, drizzled with extra virgin olive oil, if liked, and broken into individual fingers.

Minced beef, bacon and mozzarella

Safe

Apologies to any vegetarian parents out there, but this pizza made top marks at our unofficial kids' pizza taste test. What can we do?

Makes 1 pizza

1 x 30-cm (12-in) **Crispy pizza base (see page 28)**
  or 1 **Thick-crust pizza base (see page 30)**
200g (7oz) **lean beef, chicken or turkey mince**
200ml (7fl oz) **Hidden vegetable tomato sauce for kids**
  (see page 170)
3 **slices bacon**, cooked
100g (3½oz) **block mozzarella**, grated

Prepare the pizza base so it is ready to be topped. Preheat the oven to 220°C/425°F/Gas mark 7.

Heat a heavy-bottomed saucepan over medium heat. Add the mince and cook. When the meat begins to cook, break it up with a wooden spoon. Once cooked, drain off any excess fat. Set aside.

Spoon the sauce over the base leaving a 1cm (½in) border around the edge. Add the mince. Break the cooked bacon over the pizza. Finish with the grated mozzarella cheese.

Bake in the middle of the oven – 10–12 minutes for a crispy base, 12–15 for a thick crust – until the crust is golden and the cheese is bubbling. Allow to cool slightly, slice and serve immediately.

Welsh rarebit and ham pizza

Tasty

A traditional Welsh rarebit usually has beer added to it to make the mixture into more of a paste. I've modified it to be more kid-friendly by adding tomato ketchup instead.

Makes 1 pizza

1 x 25-cm (10-in) **Quick scone base (see page 29)**
125g (4oz) **Cheddar cheese,** grated
1 **onion,** grated
1–2 tsp **Dijon mustard**
3–4 splashes **Worcestershire sauce**
4 Tbsp **tomato ketchup**
100g (3½oz) **sliced ham**

Prepare the base so it is ready to be topped. Preheat the oven to 200°C/400°F/Gas mark 6.

In a bowl combine the cheese, onion, mustard, Worcestershire sauce and tomato ketchup until well mixed. Place the ham slices evenly over the base and top with the cheese mixture, spreading it almost to the edges. Cook in the middle of the preheated oven for 16–18 minutes or until lightly golden and the base is cooked. Remove from the oven and allow to cool slightly before eating.

Make your own pizza party

Joyous

Either of our quick, no-rise doughs, rolled out before a buffet of ingredients creates the easiest, happiest pizza-making party around.

Makes 4 x 15-cm (6-in) pizzas

1 quantity **Quick scone base dough or Gluten-free quick pizza base dough (see pages 29 and 34)**
Quick classic tomato sauce (see page 170)
Shop-bought barbecue sauce

All, or a selection, of the following toppings
Frankfurters, chopped into bite-sized pieces
Salami, thinly sliced
Cooked chicken breasts or ham, chopped
1 **green pepper,** cored and sliced into rings
1 **red pepper,** cored and sliced into rings
1 **small pineapple,** chopped into bite-sized pieces
Gouda, harvarti or Cheddar cheese, grated
Sweetcorn
Cherry tomatoes, sliced or halved

Preheat the oven to 220°C/425°F/Gas mark 7. Divide the pizza dough into four balls. Roll the balls, one at a time on a floured surface, into 15-cm (6-in) rounds. Place the sauces and the topping ingredients in individual bowls.

Allow children to top their own pizzas with their chosen ingredients. Transfer the pizzas to baking sheets lined with baking parchment and bake for 6–8 minutes, until the crust is golden and the cheese is bubbling. Allow to cool slightly, slice and serve.

Make your own pizza party

Hidden vegetable, tomato and havarti

Hidden vegetable, tomato and havarti
Simple

Isn't it great when fast food is actually healthy?

Makes 1 pizza

1 x 30-cm (12-in) **Crispy pizza base (see page 28)**
  or 1 **Gluten-free quick base (see page 34)**
200ml (7fl oz) **Hidden vegetable tomato sauce for kids**
  (see page 170)
150g (5oz) **Cheddar or havarti cheese,** cubed
2 **tomatoes,** thinly sliced
½ tsp **dried oregano**

Prepare your chosen pizza base so it is ready to be topped.
Preheat the oven to 220°C/425°F/Gas mark 7.

Spoon the sauce over the base leaving a 1cm (½in) border around
the edge. Scatter cubed cheese over sauce and top with sliced
tomatoes. Bake in the middle of the oven (10–12 minutes for a
crispy base, 12–15 minutes for a gluten-free base) until the crust
is golden and the cheese is bubbling. Allow to cool slightly, slice
and serve.

Sweetcorn, ham and red pepper

Smoky

This pizza, which takes its inspiration from the American Southwest, is full of texture and sweet, smoky and spicy flavours. Leftover ham is perfect for this pizza – the tastier the ham, the better the pizza! Shop-bought barbecue sauce can be used if you are short of time.

Makes 1 pizza

1 x 30-cm (12-in) **Crispy pizza base (see page 28)**
    or 1 **Thick-crust pizza base (see page 30)**
2 Tbsp **Mustard and bourbon barbecue sauce (see page 171)**
175g (6oz) **cooked ham,** torn into bite-size pieces
80g (3oz) **sweetcorn**
1 **small red pepper,** seeded and cubed
75g (2¾oz) **smoked Gouda cheese,** grated
Handful **fresh coriander leaves,** to garnish (optional)

Prepare the pizza base so it is ready to be topped. Preheat the oven to 220°C/425°F/Gas mark 7.

Spoon the barbecue sauce over the base leaving a 1cm (½in) border around the edge. Top with the ham, sweetcorn and pepper. Finish with grated cheese. Bake for 10-12 minutes for a crispy crust, 12–15 minutes for a thick crust, until the crust is golden. Garnish with coriander, if using, and serve immediately.

Sweetcorn, ham and red pepper

Sweet

Little Lindsay, my 12-year old goddaughter has tasted more recipes, either tried, true, or still being tested, than she would care to remember. She's sampled fiery spices, savoury ice creams, dark green juices, nutty burgers and pizzas, both barbecued and baked. She tastes, she swallows, and she is always honest. But little Lindsay draws the line at chocolate pizza. I wonder what she's thinking. Is that mince simmering on the stove about to be spooned over a chocolate pizza? What about the mound of grated smoked Gouda cheese? Will I have to eat it?

Not to worry, little Lindsay. This chapter is all about sweetness. Sweetened dough, sweetened topping, sweetened syrups. There may be nuts in some of the recipes, a little coconut, perhaps even a splash of sweet wine. But no mince.

Sweetness is the essence of this chapter. We've taken the traditional pizza shape and applied our favourite sweet flavours to the formula. And besides, doesn't everyone want a triangular-shaped portion of dessert?

Grape, raisin and vin santo

Viticulture

This pizza uses grapes at several different stages in their production life. They seem to just get sweeter and sweeter.

Makes 1 pizza

75g (2¾oz) **raisins**
50ml (2fl oz) **vin santo or Marsala**
1 x 30-cm (12-in) **thick crust Sweet honey pizza base**
   (see page 41)
200g (7oz) **seedless red and black grapes**
1–2 Tbsp **demerara sugar**
Mascarpone or crème fraîche, to serve (optional)

Soak the raisins in the vin santo or Marsala overnight.

Prepare the pizza base so it is ready to be topped. Preheat the oven to 220°C/425°F/Gas mark 7.

Evenly scatter the soaked raisins and grapes over the base leaving a 1–2-cm (½–¾-in) border around the edge. Sprinkle over the sugar and drizzle over any extra vin santo that was not absorbed by the raisins.

Cook in the middle of the preheated oven for 10–12 minutes or until golden and crispy. Remove from the oven and serve immediately with a dollop of mascarpone or crème fraîche on the top of each slice, if liked.

Grape, raisin and vin santo

Fig, rosemary and blue cheese

Fragrant

This pizza is really on the borderline between sweet and savoury. To go the more savoury way, omit the honey and add a handful of rocket leaves and a good grind of black pepper just before serving.

Makes 1 pizza

2 Tbsp **extra virgin olive oil**
1 **red onion,** finely sliced
1 tsp **finely chopped fresh rosemary**
150ml (5fl oz) **red wine**
100ml (3½fl oz) **balsamic vinegar**
50g (2oz) **caster sugar**
150g (5oz) **plump dried figs,** quartered
1 x 30-cm (12-in) **Crispy pizza base (see page 28)**
100g (3½oz) **Gorgonzola, dolcelatte or Stilton cheese**

Heat the oil in a non-stick frying pan or sauté pan. Add the onions and sauté until soft but not browned, about 6–8 minutes. Add the rosemary and sauté for a further minute before adding the wine and vinegar. Keep the heat at medium until the liquid has reduced by half. Add the sugar and figs and reduce the heat. Cook, stirring occasionally, for 15–20 minutes or until the mixture is the consistency of a syrupy jam. Remove from the heat and cool.

Preheat the oven to 220°C/425°F/Gas mark 7. Prepare the pizza base so it is ready to be topped. Spread the fig and rosemary preserve over the base, leaving a 1–2-cm (½–¾-in) border around the edge. Evenly scatter over chunks of the blue cheese.

Cook in the middle of the preheated oven for 10–12 minutes or until crispy and golden. Serve immediately.

Pear, pecorino and walnut

Savoury-sweet

Serve this pizza with a glass of sweet dessert wine and a few basil leaves scattered on top. This is a favourite combination of ours – featured as a salad in our *Barbecue!* book.

Makes 1 pizza

1 x 30-cm (12-in) **Crispy pizza base (see page 28)**
1 Tbsp **basil or lemon oil (plain oil will do if you don't have any)**
1 **pear,** cored and cut into slices (see Tip below)
50g (2oz) **pecorino cheese,** thinly shaved
50g (2oz) **walnut pieces**
Freshly ground black pepper
1 Tbsp **runny honey,** to serve

Prepare the pizza base so it is ready to be topped. Preheat the oven to 220°C/425°F/Gas mark 7.

Brush the basil oil, using a pastry brush, all over the base. Scatter over the pear slices, or fan them if you have time, leaving a 1–2-cm (½–¾-in) border around the edge. Then scatter over the pecorino cheese and the walnut pieces. Season lightly with black pepper. Cook in the middle of the preheated oven for 10–12 minutes or until crispy and golden. Drizzle over the honey and serve immediately.

■ *Bosc pears – large, slender pears with rust-coloured skin – hold their shape well when baked. Any pear, however, will do. Increase the quantity if the pears are small.*

Banana, chocolate and pecan

Indulgent

This is the ultimate decadent dessert.

Makes 1 pizza

130g (4½oz) **butter**
120g (4oz) **continental plain baking chocolate, chopped**
4 **eggs**
¼ tsp **salt**
300g (10oz) **caster sugar**
1 tsp **vanilla extract**
170g (6oz) **plain flour**

For the topping
1 **banana**
Juice of 1 **lemon**
100ml (3½fl oz) **soured cream or mascarpone**
¼ tsp **nutmeg**
12–15 **pecan nuts**
1 Tbsp **demerara sugar**

Preheat the oven to 180°C/350°F/Gas mark 4. Put the butter and chocolate in a heatproof bowl set over a pan of simmering water. Stir occasionally, until melted. Set aside to cool. Beat the eggs with the salt in an electric mixer until pale.

Slowly add the sugar with the beaters going, until the mixture is light and fluffy. Stir in the vanilla and the chocolate mixture and beat until smooth. Fold in the flour until combined.

Put the banana, lemon juice, soured cream and nutmeg in a bowl and mash together.

Line a 36 x 41-cm (14 x 16-in) baking sheet with baking parchment. Spoon the chocolate mixture on to the parchment and spread into a 30-cm (12-in) circle. Using a teaspoon, randomly spoon the banana mixture over the chocolate pizza base, as if topping a pizza. Press the topping gently into the base. Scatter over the pecans and sugar.

Bake in the centre of the oven for 25 minutes, until cooked through in the centre, but still very moist. Cool, slice and serve.

Cranberry, orange and mascarpone

Festive

This festive, colourfully sweet pizza is delicious with a glass of white wine and a sampling of cheeses.

Makes 1 pizza

1 x 30-cm (12-in) **thick crust Sweet honey pizza base (see page 41),** with the saffron omitted and substituting orange rind for the lemon
300g (10oz) **cranberries,** fresh or frozen
75ml (2½fl oz) **orange juice**
100g (3½oz) **caster sugar**
2 Tbsp **walnuts,** chopped
200g (7oz) **mascarpone**

Preheat the oven to 200°C/400°F/Gas mark 6. Prepare the pizza base so it is ready for topping and set aside.

Put the cranberries in a medium-sized saucepan over medium heat. Add the orange juice and sugar, stir and simmer the berries for 10–12 minutes, until they begin to pop (let them simmer a few minutes longer if using frozen cranberries). Remove the pan from the heat. Stir in the walnuts and 100g (3½oz) mascarpone into the cranberry mixture. Spoon the rest of the mascarpone over the pizza base. Top with the cranberry mixture.

Bake for 12 minutes, until the crust is golden and cooked through. Cool slightly, slice and serve.

Apple, sultana and cinnamon strudel

Spiced

Is it a calzone or an apple turnover? You could be forgiven for thinking either.

Makes 2 pizza strudels

½ quantity **Sweet honey pizza base dough (see page 41)**
2–3 (about 500g/1lb 2oz) **apples,** peeled, cored and sliced
Juice of 1 **lemon**
4 Tbsp **sultanas**
2 Tbsp **brandy**
1 tsp **cinnamon**
½ tsp **ground nutmeg**
2 Tbsp **caster sugar** (optional)
2 Tbsp **melted butter**
2 Tbsp **brown sugar**
Pouring cream, to serve

Preheat the oven to 220°C/425°F/Gas mark 7. Divide the dough into two and roll each out into 30-cm (12-in) rounds, on baking parchment, and leave to rest for about 10 minutes.

In a bowl combine the apple slices, lemon juice, sultanas, brandy, cinnamon, ground nutmeg and sugar if using, and mix to combine. Leave to rest for about 5 minutes then drain and scatter the apple slices and sultanas over one half of the base, leaving 2cm (¾in) as a rim. Pull the uncovered half of dough up and over the filling and, using your fingers, crimp the edge to seal it forming a crescent shape. Prick the top once or twice with a fork, brush with the melted butter and sprinkle over the brown sugar.

Carefully transfer the baking parchment to a baking sheet and cook for about 15 minutes, or until golden and the base is cooked through. Allow to rest for a few minutes before serving with pouring cream.

Apple, sultana and cinnamon strudel

Chocolate brownie

Chocolate brownie

Decadent

It's a wonderful thing when favourite flavours come together in one, perfect circle.

Makes 1 pizza

130g (4½oz) **butter**
120g (4oz) **continental plain baking chocolate, chopped**
4 **eggs**
¼ tsp **salt**
300g (10oz) **caster sugar**
1 tsp **vanilla extract**
170g (6oz) **plain flour**

For the topping
150g (5oz) **cream cheese,** at room temperature
50g (2oz) **sweet desiccated coconut**
50g (2oz) **chocolate chips, or plain chocolate, roughly chopped**

Preheat the oven to 180°C/350°F/Gas mark 4. Put the butter and chocolate in a heatproof bowl set over a pan of simmering water. Stir occasionally, until melted. Set aside to cool.

Beat the eggs with the salt in an electric mixer until pale. Slowly add the sugar with the beaters going, until the mixture is light and fluffy. Stir in the vanilla and the chocolate mixture and beat until smooth. Fold in the flour until combined.

Put the cream cheese, coconut and chocolate chips in a bowl. Mash the mixture with a fork until combined.

Line a 36 x 41-cm (14 x 16-in) baking sheet with baking parchment. Spoon the chocolate mixture on to parchment and spread into a 30-cm (12-in) circle. Using a teaspoon, randomly spoon the cream cheese mixture over the chocolate pizza base, as if topping a pizza. Press the topping lightly into the chocolate base. Bake in the centre of the oven for 25 minutes, until the centre is cooked, but still very moist. Cool, slice and serve.

Pear pizza tatin

Comfort

Tarte Tatin, the classic French upside-down tart, is traditionally made with caramelized apples and topped with puff pastry and baked in the oven. Here, Tarte Tatin enters the pizza world featuring pears, cranberries and pecans all caramelized together with a sweet pizza crust. It's the perfect festive brunch fare.

Makes 1 pizza

1 **thin crust Sweet honey pizza base (see page 41),** with the saffron omitted
800g (1lb 10oz) **pears,** peeled, cored and quartered
½ tsp **Chinese 5 spice**
130g (4½oz) **caster sugar**
2 Tbsp **butter**
2 Tbsp **cranberries (optional)**
Handful **pecans**

Preheat the oven to 180°C/ 350°F/Gas mark 4. Prepare the pizza base, rolling it out to approximately 25cm (10in) in diameter and set aside.

In a large bowl toss the pear quarters with the Chinese 5 spice. Put the sugar in a 24-cm (9½-in) diameter, 4.5cm (1¾-in) deep ovenproof frying pan. Scatter the butter over the sugar. Arrange pears in a snug circle around the pan, cut sides facing in the same direction. Tuck the remaining pears inside the circle. Scatter the cranberries and pecans between the pears. Heat the pan over medium–medium-high heat. Juices will bubble. Continue to cook, shaking the pan to loosen the contents every so often, until the juices have caramelized to a dark golden colour, about 30 minutes. Watch carefully so it doesn't burn. Remove from the heat, but leave contents in the pan.

Place the pizza base over the pears in the pan, tucking the edges of the base inside the pan. Bake for 10 minutes, cover with foil and bake for 15 minutes more. Invert the pan onto a serving platter. Cool slightly, slice and serve.

Pear pizza tatin

Sauces

Pesto

Pesto was invented by the Genoese as a vehicle for the much abundant and much loved herb, basil. Traditionally it was made from olive oil, garlic, pine nuts, butter and grated Parmesan cheese. These days pesto has taken on a whole new meaning and covers a whole range of sauces acting as a vehicle for one dominant ingredient such as walnuts, rocket and red peppers. On pages 162–165 are a few of our favourite interpretations of pesto.

Basil pesto

Makes 250ml (8fl oz)

1 large bunch (about 60–80g/2¼–3oz) **basil, leaves only**
2 **cloves garlic, peeled and chopped**
50g (2oz) **finely grated Parmesan cheese**
50g (2oz) **pine nuts**
About 150–200ml (5–7fl oz) **extra virgin olive oil**

Put the basil, garlic, Parmesan and pine nuts and a good splosh of the olive oil in a food processor and whizz until blended. With the motor still running, slowly add the remaining olive oil through the feed tube until the desired consistency is reached. Transfer to a jar or airtight container and cover with a thin layer of oil. Seal and refrigerate for up to 2 weeks.

Parsley pesto

Makes 250ml (8fl oz)

1 large bunch (about 60–80g/2¼–3oz) **flat-leaf parsley**
1 **clove garlic,** peeled and roughly chopped
50g (2oz) **finely grated Parmesan cheese**
50g (2oz) **pine nuts**
Grated rind of 1 **lemon**
About 150–200ml (5–7fl oz) **extra virgin olive oil**
Salt and freshly ground black pepper to taste

Put the parsley, garlic, Parmesan, pine nuts and lemon rind in a food processor with about a quarter of the olive oil. Whizz to a coarse purée. With the motor still running, drizzle in the remaining olive oil until the desired consistency is reached. Season the pesto with salt and pepper. Parmesan cheese varies in saltiness so it is important to taste the pesto first before seasoning. Transfer to a jar or airtight container and cover with a thin layer of oil. Seal and refrigerate for up to 2 weeks.

Rocket pesto

Makes 250ml (8fl oz)

60–80g (2¼–3oz) **rocket leaves**
1 **clove garlic,** crushed
50g (2oz) **finely grated Parmesan cheese**
50g (2oz) **pine nuts**
150–200ml (7fl oz) **extra virgin olive oil**
Sea salt and freshly ground black pepper to taste

Put the rocket, garlic, Parmesan and pine nuts in a food processor with about a quarter of the olive oil. Whizz to a coarse purée. With the motor still running, drizzle in the remaining olive oil until the desired consistency is reached. Season – Parmesan varies in saltiness so it is important to taste the pesto before seasoning. Transfer to an airtight container and cover with a thin layer of oil. Seal and refrigerate for up to 2 weeks.

Walnut pesto

Makes 250ml (8fl oz)

2 **cloves garlic**, peeled and roughly chopped
50g (2oz) **grated Parmesan cheese**
100g (3½oz) **fresh shelled walnuts**
125–150ml (4–5fl oz) **extra virgin olive oil**
1 **handful basil leaves**, torn
Salt and freshly ground black pepper to taste

Put the garlic, Parmesan, walnuts and a good splosh of olive oil in a food processor and whizz to a paste. With the motor still running, drizzle in the remaining olive oil until the desired consistency is reached. Tear up the basil into the food processor and blitz once or twice to combine but do not whizz to completely purée the basil. Add salt and pepper. Transfer to a jar or airtight container and cover with a thin layer of olive oil. Seal and refrigerate for up to 2 weeks.

Coriander pesto

Makes 250ml (8fl oz)

2 **cloves garlic**, peeled and roughly chopped
3 Tbsp **grated Parmesan cheese**
25g (1oz) **fresh shelled walnuts**
1 **red chilli,** halved, with stem and seeds removed
75ml (2½fl oz) **extra virgin olive oil**
40g (1½oz) **coriander**
10g (½oz) **mint**
10g (¼oz) **chives**
Grated rind of 1 **lime**
Juice of ½ **lime**
Salt and freshly ground black pepper to taste

Put the garlic, Parmesan, walnuts, chilli and 1 Tbsp of the olive oil in a food processor and whizz to a paste. With the motor still running, drizzle in the remaining olive oil until the desired consistency is reached. Add the herbs, lime rind and juice to the food processor and blitz to combine but do not whizz to completely purée the herbs. Add salt and pepper to taste. Transfer to a jar or airtight container and cover with a thin layer of oil. Seal and refrigerate for up to 2 weeks.

Roasted red pepper and olive pesto

Makes 250ml (8fl oz)

40g (1½oz) **sun-dried tomatoes**, (dry – not packed in oil)
1 **small red pepper**, roasted, peeled, deseeded and roughly chopped
5 **kalamata olives**, stoned and roughly chopped
5g (⅙oz) **flat-leaf parsley**
5g (⅙oz) **basil**
20g (¾oz) **grated Parmesan cheese**
2 **cloves garlic**, crushed
2 Tbsp **extra virgin olive oil**
½ tsp **balsamic vinegar**
Sea salt and ground black pepper to taste

Put the sun-dried tomatoes in a small bowl and cover with boiling water. Leave to soften for 20 minutes. Drain water, pushing as much liquid from the sun-dried tomatoes as possible. Place them in a food processor with the chopped red pepper, olives, parsley, basil, Parmesan and garlic. Pulse until the mixture is roughly chopped. Add the olive oil and balsamic vinegar and continue to pulse until coarse, but spreadable. Add salt and pepper to taste. Cover the pesto with a thin layer of olive oil. Seal and refrigerate for up to 2 weeks.

Sun-dried tomato pesto

Makes 125ml (4fl oz)

30g (1¼oz) **sun-dried tomatoes**
75ml (2½fl oz) **red wine vinegar**
50ml (2fl oz) **balsamic vinegar**
3 **cloves garlic**, crushed
1 tsp **caster sugar**
75ml (2½fl oz) **extra virgin olive oil**
Sea salt and pepper to taste

Place the sun-dried tomatoes and both vinegars in a small saucepan and bring to a gentle simmer. Remove from the heat and allow to sit for 5 minutes, until the sun-dried tomatoes are slightly softened. Pour the sun-dried tomatoes and vinegars into a food processor. Add the garlic, sugar and olive oil and pulse until roughly blended. Add salt and pepper to taste. Use immediately, or transfer to a jar or airtight container and cover with a thin layer of olive oil. Seal and refrigerate for up to 2 weeks.

Slow-roasted tomatoes

The intense flavour of the tomatoes becomes very concentrated after long, slow cooking. When tomatoes are in season you may not even need to add any sugar. Make more than you need and preserve them in oil until needed.

Makes enough for 1–2 pizzas

800g (1lb 12oz) medium-sized plum tomatoes
1 Tbsp extra virgin olive oil
1 tsp caster sugar
½ tsp dried oregano

Preheat the oven to 120°C/250°F/Gas mark ½. Cut the tomatoes in half lengthways and scoop out the seeds. Place the tomatoes, cut-side up, on a baking sheet and drizzle over the oil. Evenly sprinkle over the sugar and oregano and put in the oven. Roast the tomatoes for 2–2½ hours or until semi-dried. Remove from the oven, cool and store in an airtight container for 3–4 days in the fridge. Alternatively, cover completely in extra virgin olive oil, seal in a sterilized jar and keep for up to 2 months.

Slow-roasted tomato sauce

Makes enough for 1–2 pizzas

1 quantity **Slow-roasted tomatoes** (see page 166)
Handful **basil leaves**
1–2 **cloves garlic,** roughly chopped
2 Tbsp **extra virgin olive oil**

Put the roasted tomatoes in a food processor or, alternatively, grind by hand using a mortar and pestle. Add the basil leaves, garlic and olive oil. Pulse or grind to a coarse paste. This sauce can be stored in the fridge in an airtight container for up to 1 week.

Sweet cherry tomato sauce

Makes enough for 2 pizzas

800g (1lb 12oz) **cherry tomatoes,** halved
2 **cloves garlic,** sliced
2 **sprigs rosemary,** leaves only
1 Tbsp **runny honey**
1 Tbsp **extra virgin olive oil**
Sea salt and freshly ground black pepper to taste

Preheat the oven to 200°C/400°F/Gas mark 6. Place the tomatoes, cut-side up, on a baking sheet. Sprinkle over the garlic slices and rosemary sprigs then evenly drizzle over the honey and oil. Season with salt and pepper and roast in the oven for 10–12 minutes or until the tomatoes are bursting and juicy. Allow to cool before tipping the tomatoes and all the juices into an airtight container. This sauce can be refrigerated in an airtight container for up to 3–4 days.

Spicy tomato sauce

Remove the chilli flakes for a more classic, concentrated, cooked tomato sauce.

Makes 650ml (1¼pt)

2 Tbsp **olive oil**
1 **large onion,** finely chopped
3 **cloves garlic,** peeled
1 tsp **dried oregano**
½–1 tsp **dried chilli flakes**
2 x 400-g (14-oz) **tins chopped tomatoes**

Heat the oil in a large saucepan. Add the onion and sauté for 2–3 minutes or until translucent but not browned. Add the garlic, oregano and chilli flakes and sauté for a further 1–2 minutes, stirring occasionally. Add the tinned tomatoes and bring to the boil, stirring. Reduce the heat and simmer for about 25 minutes or until richly red and concentrated, stirring occasionally. Allow to cool and store in the fridge, in an airtight container, for up to 1 week.

Tomato and roasted red pepper sauce

This pizza sauce is based on a Croatian sauce called *Ajvar*. My friend, Sarah Carlyle, and I managed to add it to every meal as we camped our way along the Croatian coast. I've invented my own version and decided it is just as suited to pizza.

Makes 500ml (18fl oz) – enough for 4 pizzas

3 **large red peppers,** halved and deseeded
600g (1lb 5oz) **tomatoes,** halved
¼–½ tsp **dried chilli flakes**
2 **cloves garlic,** sliced
2 Tbsp **extra virgin olive oil**

Preheat the oven to 200°C/400°F/Gas mark 6. Place the red pepper, cut-side down, on a baking sheet and roast for about 25–30 minutes or until starting to blacken. Put the tomatoes, cut-side up, on a separate sheet and sprinkle over the dried chilli flakes and garlic slices then drizzle over the olive oil. Add to the oven after about 10 minutes after the peppers and roast for 15–20 minutes. When the peppers are ready, remove from the oven and leave until cool enough to handle. Peel off the skin and put the flesh in a food processor. Add the tomatoes and all the juices and process in bursts until blended but not too smooth. Allow to cool then store in the fridge, in an airtight container, for up to 1 week.

Black olive tapénade

Makes 250ml (8fl oz)

170g (6oz) **stoned black olives,** drained
50g (2oz) **anchovy fillets**
2 Tbsp **capers,** rinsed
50ml (2fl oz) **extra virgin olive oil**
Freshly ground black pepper to taste

Put the olives, anchovies and capers in the bowl of a food processor and pulse to combine. With the motor running, pour in the oil through the feed tube. Season to taste with freshly ground black pepper. Transfer to a jar, cover with a thin layer of oil and refrigerate for up to 2 weeks.

Caramelized fennel relish

Makes enough for 1–2 pizzas

1 Tbsp **extra virgin olive oil**
1 **onion,** thinly sliced
1 **large bulb fennel,** very thinly sliced
1 **clove garlic,** crushed
4 Tbsp **caster sugar**
1 Tbsp **whole-grain mustard**
2 Tbsp **white wine vinegar or cider vinegar**
Salt and freshly ground black pepper to taste

Heat the oil in a non-stick saucepan over medium heat and add the onion, fennel and garlic. Stir until well coated in the oil, and the onion and fennel start to soften but not brown. Increase the heat, add the sugar and stir constantly for a further 2– 3 minutes, or until starting to brown. Stir in the mustard and vinegar and season generously with salt and pepper. When the liquid has evaporated, reduce the heat slightly and leave the mixture to caramelize and darken around the edges, stirring occasionally, for a further 8–12 minutes. Set aside to cool. This relish can be made up to 3 days in advance and kept for up to 1 week stored in an airtight container in the fridge.

Quick classic tomato sauce

This is an excellent sauce to have on hand – it takes seconds to make, and keeps for up to 1 week in the fridge or up to 3 months in the freezer. Experiment with the amount of spice to suit your taste.

Makes 500ml (18fl oz)

796-ml (1¼-pt) **tin tomatoes**, well drained
3 Tbsp **tomato purée**
1 tsp **dried basil**
1 tsp **dried oregano**
½ tsp **caster sugar**
½ tsp **salt**
½ tsp **dried chilli flakes**
½ tsp **crushed black pepper**
2 **cloves garlic**, finely chopped (optional)

Combine all ingredients in a food processor and blend until smooth. Transfer to a small bowl or measuring jug and use immediately, or cover and either refrigerate for up to 1 week or freeze.

Hidden vegetable tomato sauce for kids

This mild-flavoured sauce is the perfect way to pack nutrients into your children's pizza. Spoon it over a base, top with cheese – et voilà, a healthy, simple meal.

Makes 1L (1¾pt)

800-g (1lb 12-oz) **tin tomatoes**, drained
150g (5oz) **courgettes**, roughly chopped
150g (5oz) **carrots**, peeled and roughly chopped
200g (7oz) **baby spinach**
200g (7oz) **onion**, peeled and roughly chopped
2 **cloves garlic**, crushed
½ tsp **salt**

Combine all the ingredients in a food processor and blend until roughly chopped. (Take it further if you think the vegetables are too visible!) Pour the sauce into a large saucepan and simmer, uncovered, for 40 minutes, stirring frequently, until the sauce has reduced by half. Use 150–200ml (5–7fl oz) of sauce for a 30-cm (12-in) pizza. Freeze any remaining sauce in an airtight container for up to 6 months.

Caramelized onions

1 Tbsp **olive oil**
1 Tbsp **butter**
2 **large onions,** thinly sliced
Salt and freshly ground pepper to taste
½ tsp **anchovy paste (optional)**

Heat the olive oil and butter in a large frying pan over medium-high heat. Add the onions and reduce the heat to low. Sauté until softened, stirring occasionally. Add a sprinkling of salt and pepper, but not too much salt, as the anchovy paste will add a salty kick. Continue to sauté over low heat, stirring occasionally, until brown and caramelized, 20–30 minutes. Mix in the anchovy paste (if using), stir, and remove from heat. These onions can be kept in the fridge for up to 1 week.

Mustard bourbon barbecue sauce

It doesn't get much better than this rich, sweet yet smoky, decadent sauce. The sauce will keep, covered, for up to 3 weeks in the fridge, or store it in an airtight container in the freezer for up to 6 months.

Makes 750ml (1¼pt)

1 tsp **vegetable oil**
1 bunch **spring onions,** chopped
1 **medium white onion,** chopped
4 **large cloves garlic,** chopped
200g (7oz) **packed golden brown sugar**
125ml (4fl oz) **tomato ketchup**
75ml (2½fl oz) **tomato purée**
125ml (4fl oz) **whole-grain Dijon mustard**
125ml (4fl oz) **water**
75ml (2½fl oz) **Worcestershire sauce**
75ml (2½fl oz) **cider vinegar**
75ml (2½fl oz) **apple juice**
1 **chipotle chilli in adobo sauce,** finely chopped
1 tsp **ground cumin**
350ml (12fl oz) **bourbon or whisky**
Salt and freshly ground black pepper to taste

Heat the oil in a heavy large pan over medium-low heat. Add the spring onions, white onion and garlic and sauté until tender, about 15 minutes. Mix in the remaining ingredients, adding the bourbon last. Simmer the sauce until thick and reduced to 750ml (1¼pt), stirring occasionally, for about 1 hour. Season to taste with salt and pepper. This sauce can be prepared 2 weeks in advance. Cover and refrigerate.

About the authors

Pippa Cuthbert is a New Zealander living and working in London. Ever since childhood she has been passionate about food, cooking and eating! Pippa discovered her passion for wood-fired pizzas while working on cookery courses in Tuscany with Ursula Ferrigno. Her passion for simple, fresh and seasonal produce comes through in her work. After studying Nutrition and Food Science at Otago University in New Zealand and working in the Test Kitchen of Nestlé New Zealand she decided to travel the world in search of new and exciting culinary adventures. Pippa has been living in London for over five years and is working predominantly as a food stylist and food writer. She works on books, magazines, TV commercials, advertising, packaging and PR.

Canadian born Lindsay Cameron Wilson is never far from a pizza paddle. When out of reach, she's writing. She blended her passion for food and writing at University where she studied History, Journalism and the Culinary Arts. In 2001 she left her job as a food columnist in Halifax, Nova Scotia and moved to London. It was there where she met Pippa at Books for Cooks in Notting Hill and shortly after the work on their first book, *Juice!* began. Fuelled by juice, the two moved on to *Ice Cream!*, *Soup!*, *Barbecue!* and now *Pizza!* In 2004 Lindsay returned to Canada with her husband James and son Luke, where she continues to work as a food journalist.

Bibliography

Amandonico, Nikko, *La Pizza,* Mitchell Beazley, 2001
David, Elizabeth, *Italian Food,* Penguin, 1963
David, Elizabeth, *English Bread and Yeast Cookery*, Penguin, 2001
Ferrigno, Ursula & Trieulle, Eric, *Bread,* (Dorling Kindersley, 1988) Harzan,
Marcella, *The Essentials of Classic Italian Cooking,* Macmillan, 1992
McGee, Harold, *On Food and Cooking,* Simon & Schuster Inc, 1984
Steingarten, Jeffrey, *It Must've Been Something I Ate*, Vintage Books, 2003

Index